From
the
Grassroots

From the Grassroots

A History
of United Methodist
Volunteers In Mission

Thomas L. Curtis, Sr.

WITH MARY EGERTON HIGGS

Abingdon Press
Nashville

FROM THE GRASSROOTS
A HISTORY OF UNITED METHODIST VOLUNTEERS IN MISSION

Library of Congress Cataloging-in-Publication Data

Curtis, Thomas L., 1931-
    From the grassroots: a history of United Methodist Volunteers In Mission/
Thomas L. Curtis.
        p. cm.
    Includes bibliographical references.
    ISBN 0-687-07520-3 (alk. paper)
    1. United Methodist Volunteers in Mission—History. I. Title.

    BV2550.C87 2000
    267'.1876—dc21   00-026737

00 01 02 03 04 05 06 07 08 09—10 9 8 7 6 5 4 3 2 1

MANUFACTURED IN THE UNITED STATES OF AMERICA

*To Dr. Mike Watson,
beloved UMVIM pioneer
who has shepherded
this ministry since its beginning
in the early seventies,
and to the many thousands
of volunteers
who are the heartbeat
of this grassroots movement*

Foreword

The United Methodist Volunteers In Mission movement, and the entire United Methodist Church, owe Tom and Margaret Curtis a huge debt of gratitude. In less than twenty years they took an organization in its embryonic state and guided and developed it into what the chief executive of the General Board of Global Ministries has called the "most rapidly growing mission organization in the world."

Tom and Margaret didn't simply work with this volunteer program; they lived it. They were totally immersed in it, and this shows in the amazing record of accomplishment.

When I think of the task that confronted them when they started to write this account, the nearest comparison I can make is to imagine trying to pick up spilled mercury with your fingers. This grassroots movement was progressing in so many areas of our country as well as in other lands at the same time that it makes my head swim to imagine how it could be written down in a coherent manner. Yet Tom has produced a book that is accurate and readable and still catches the excitement that has characterized this ministry since its beginning.

I invite you to read for yourself the marvelous story of the unfolding of this movement, which will surely be a most significant chapter when the history of our denomination is written.

Michael C. Watson, M.D.

Contents

The supreme aim of mission is to make the Lord Jesus Christ known to all people in all lands as their divine Savior... to enlist them in the Kingdom of God to cooperate with these churches to promote Christian fellowship and bring to bear on all human life the spirit and principles of God.

(from a Service of Commissioning and Recognition of Missionaries, General Board of Global Ministries, The United Methodist Church)

This project was undertaken at the request of the UMVIM-SEJ Board of Directors in cooperation with UMVIM Coordinators in all five jurisdictions of The United Methodist Church, and with the General Board of Global Ministries.

Prologue

And Jesus came and said to them, "All authority in heaven and on earth has been given to me. Go therefore and make disciples of all nations, baptizing them in the name of the Father and of the Son and of the Holy Spirit, teaching them to observe all that I have commanded you; and lo, I am with you always, to the close of the age."

Matthew 28:18-20 (RSV)

How does one talk or write about the beginning of a movement like UMVIM, United Methodist Volunteers In Mission, that goes back to the time of Jesus? One place to begin is with the Great Commission given by Jesus, which is often referred to as the church's marching orders to proclaim the gospel. To emphasize that this was a mandate that demanded obedience would only be part of the story. First-century Christians were compelled by the sheer joy of their new-found reality in the resurrected Christ. Their joy was the motivation that sent them forth to share their faith wherever they went. And these disciples were all volunteers, having to maintain their own basic support.

Saint Paul could well be considered the greatest volunteer in mission. He referred to the work of his hands as supplying his own needs and those of his companions as they traveled and preached through much of the known world. In dealing with this theme in an address to the second UMVIM-SEJ Rally in 1981, G. Ross Freeman, SEJ Executive Secretary, said, "The movemental character of Christianity dates back to the Great Commission. Today, one of its most powerful expressions is to be found in the Volunteers In Mission movement." Freeman also quoted the Reverend Michael Harper of the Anglican Church, who said, "Laymen are indispensable to the work of spreading the gospel. If they are not sufficiently involved, the church will die."

Throughout Christian history, various groups and organizations have flourished with the spirit of volunteerism. In the Methodist Church's popular Caravan movement of the 1940s and 1950s, young people traveled the country on short-term mission assignments. "The Brothers Ten" seminarians from Boston University School of Theology served in Mexico in the 1940s on summer mission projects sponsored by the American Friends Service Committee and the Methodist Board of Missions. Thus the United Methodist Volunteers In Mission movement of today does not claim to be unique in that respect. We follow in the line of a great tradition.

One of the most creative mission thinkers early in the twentieth century was the Reverend Roland Allen, a priest of the Church of England whose ideas did not begin to influence church policy until years after his death. Now more than ever his words relate to our times.

Allen gave so much prominence to the role of the laity in the cause of witnessing for Christ that eventually he gave up his ordination. He was joined by other prominent churchmen in the London Missionary Society who, he said, were "united in the conviction that a revolution was overdue in missionary work, not only in methods and principles but also in the objective itself of reaching people with the Gospel" (*Ministry of the Spirit: Selected Writings of Roland Allen* [London: World Dominion Press, 1960]). As a group they were in advance of their time; they had to wait for general recognition until "the Ecumenical Movement had taught us not merely to cooperate but to welcome the cross-fertilization of ideas between different Christian traditions."

Allen insisted that the call to mission is "independent of any training which the man [or woman] may, or may not, receive, and independent of any stipend which he [or she] may, or may not, receive." In other words, for him the call to mission comes to all Christians. The training and sending forth do not of themselves make one a missionary. As to continuing as an effective missionary, he declared, "A missionary who can only be kept a missionary by being kept in a professional ring is spiritually a failure. So outside the professional body some might fail; but that is no reason for timidity" (*Ministry of the Spirit*). This same understanding of the call to mission of all believers prevails in the volunteer movement of our day.

Prior to World War II, laypersons participated almost entirely at the local level of mission, focusing on ministry and maintenance. The impression was given that mission work was the domain of professionals. Amateurs with little experience, it was thought, would *at best* make only limited contributions, *at worst* get in the way and cause problems.

A brief survey of mission history since the close of World War II reveals the background for the rise of volunteerism in the late twentieth century. The burgeoning postwar economy brought new and unexpected sources of income to many churches, resulting in a major increase in opportunities to bring new mission projects into being. By 1968, mission agencies found themselves in a new situation vis-à-vis the national churches abroad. Overseas churches that had been recipients of mission help were forming their own mission programs. No longer simply receivers, they now were sending out their own missionaries. It would be expecting too much to think that mission executives could see the full picture of what was to come.

Bishop S. Clifton Ives of West Virginia tells of his own frustration in seeking an avenue for short-term volunteer service. "While in my first appointment in the 1960s, I wrote to the Board of Missions suggesting that mission interpretation could be increased by giving laypersons a one- or two-week experience at a mission site. I was informed that such would not be possible since there was a process all missionaries needed to go through before going into the mission field. In essence, I was told that a missionary is a professional in service for the church and that volunteers would not work in the system. Things have changed in thirty years. The Board of Global Ministries is now solidly behind Volunteers In Mission. Little did I know that others were also making similar requests. A dozen years later, standing in another pulpit, I made a plea for someone in our congregation to join a team going to Haiti under sponsorship of our annual conference and the University of Maine. After the service, a young man expressed his interest, and the congregation agreed to support him. Within a year a professor at a local college organized a group in our church to go to Haiti. I agreed to accompany them. When my two college-age children heard that I was going, they chose to go with us. We set out after Christmas on a trip that would alter our lives forever. But more important are the changed lives, the experiences of cultural diversity and the opportunities of faith development that occur through Volunteers In Mission. I am happy to be one of the thousands of persons who have found UMVIM to be an opportunity to express their faith and commitment to Jesus Christ."

Dr. Paul A. Hopkins, a senior Presbyterian mission leader, in a perceptive analysis in the late 1970s claimed, "Right at this point the mission agencies exhibited a lack of 'surefootedness' as they began to work in new and often tense relationships" (*What Next in Mission?* [Philadelphia: Westminster Press, 1977]). The massively increasing available funds were given directly to the mission agency itself and through the agency to the national churches. This in effect moved the power away from missionaries on overseas assignments to the agency at home. New and difficult strains were placed on the agency, national colleague churches, missionaries, and constituent supporting churches. Hopkins observed, "The very fact that power had flowed into agency hands [and away from missionaries] soon made it apparent that the mission agency itself was the problem."

From this vantage point, one can understand the mindset that had developed with certain mission leaders, which left little room for the spontaneous enthusiasm brought to the fore by the fledgling volunteer movement. This ministry was outside the list of priorities of most established mission agencies and had to win acceptance, however gradually, through its own momentum. I was told by senior mission officials on more than one occasion that the volunteer ministry was "not one of our priorities."

Fortunately, the United Methodist Committee on Relief (UMCOR), one of the divisions of the General Board of Global Ministries (GBGM), was readily open to different types of volunteers and, in fact, used many of them to work on disaster relief emergencies. One highly respected member of the UMCOR division was Dr. Michael Watson of Bamberg, South Carolina, who had long sought to open a channel through our church for a volunteer movement—at the time only a vision shared by a few. Before UMVIM was organized, Dr. Harry Haines, UMCOR's director, said to Dr. Watson, "Go to Haiti and see what your South Carolina doctors can do." After making his first visit to this impoverished island, Mike asked, "What do you do for a people who need everything and need it desperately and need it now?"

Dr. Watson tells of some of his initial work in Haiti, which influenced much of the development of the UMVIM movement. He and his brother, Joe Cal, an agriculturalist who soon developed a great love of Haitians, learned that UMCOR had sent Maggie Doyle, an American nurse, to a remote corner of Jeremie; but her only means of transportation was her feet. Joe reported to Mike, "Maggie has to walk everywhere she goes, and she wants a horse to ride so she can go faster and farther each day. The horse will cost about $200." Mike replied that he knew an active Sunday school class that would give that much. The only problem was how to get a saddle. Joe called a saddlemaker friend and poured out the story of Maggie's dilemma, only to hear the voice on the other end say, "I've been trying to interrupt you for several minutes. You have the wrong number. But I do want to give Maggie that saddle!"

As a physician, Dr. Watson was overwhelmed by the desperate conditions throughout the country. "One thing that distressed me most," he said, "was that 40 percent of newborns did not survive their first month of life, but died of neonatal tetanus. I also knew that if a woman was immunized against tetanus, her offspring were immune from tetanus for at least five years. So we organized a tetanus immunization program as a beginning for our medical work. At the opening clinic, so many people pressed in to receive their inoculations that they were passing young children over their heads as they feared our supplies would run out." From this small beginning has come a steady flow of volunteers to Haiti, a land now much beloved by thousands of volunteers from across the USA and elsewhere.

The major thrust of interest in volunteer service was coming from the southeast United States and other scattered parts of the country, without the active support or encouragement of principal mission leaders. Individual laypersons and clergy were taking it upon themselves to investigate and respond to the perceived need for workers, with an eagerness to get directly involved. This grass-roots concept of going out to serve as volunteers came to be known as "personalizing Christian mission."

Often this response took the form of teams of medical and building volunteers with their special skills—evangelists, teachers, agriculturists and persons with no real technical skills at all. While much mission activity took place outside the USA, many groups have given themselves to worthy projects at home, such as new church construction, disaster relief, repair of homes for disadvantaged persons, and programs for children and youth. The number of domestic teams has far exceeded the number that have served beyond our borders. Domestic teams usually just get less publicity.

Phil Amerson, an Indiana pastor and sociologist, said, "The emergence of the volunteer phenomenon suggests a redistribution of resources and power as well as new linkage in the way communities and societies function. 'Volunteers' also suggests a freedom on the part of persons to act in new ways. This is a movement from emphasis on self-directed goals to other-directed goals."

In the 1960s and 1970s, interest in voluntary mission service began to accelerate at the local level. Sometimes this was due to a pastor who had been in seminary with a person from another part of the world and received an invitation to go to that country to help on some project. Sometimes Christian laymen and laywomen on vacation were confronted with enormous needs in the community they were visiting and felt a compelling need to help. A number of conferences were proceeding on their own with the selection and placement of volunteers at home and abroad. This was especially true in the Florida, Holston, South Carolina and Western North Carolina Conferences.

By the mid-seventies, the concept of volunteers in mission had caught on so well in the Southeastern Jurisdiction that leaders of the movement came together and made plans for an office of coordination. Since that time, all annual conferences in the SEJ have organized their own committees and task forces to provide guidance to prospective volunteers in concert with the jurisdictional office.

Numbers can tell only a small but important part of any story. Let me simply report that when Margaret and I came to UMVIM as coordinators in 1976 (no other such office existed at that time in our denomination), fifty or so teams (with perhaps a total of 600 team members in all) and a few individuals had worked through the SEJ Office of Coordination. In 1994, a total of 9,520 volunteers from the Southeastern Jurisdiction alone went out on UMVIM mission projects and contributed $3,832,000 to mission in that year, an amount which reflected an increase every year since the office opened.

In 1997, reports from all five jurisdictions showed a continuing increase in the number of volunteers serving and their financial contributions as reflected in the following table:

	North Central	Northeastern	South Central	Southeastern	Western
Volunteers	8,500	2,332	10,183	11,442	4,100
Contributions	$3,200,000	$2,180,900	$3,637,892	$6,114,594	$850,000

Countries served that year included Antigua, Armenia, Belize, Bolivia, Bosnia, Brazil, Chile, Costa Rica, Cuba, Czech Republic, Dominican Republic, El Salvador, England, Estonia, Guatemala, Haiti, Honduras, Israel, Jamaica, Kazakhstan, Kenya, Liberia, Lithuania, Macedonia, Mexico, Montserrat, Mozambique, Nicaragua, Nigeria, Palestinian Territories, Panama, Philippines, Poland, Puerto Rico, Georgia (Republic of), Russia, St. Maarten, St. Vincent, Sierra Leone, Slovakia, South Africa, USA, and Zimbabwe.

Countless thousands of lives have been touched by this everexpanding ministry. Many Advance Special projects have been completed through the efforts of volunteers and the contributions of their home congregations who supported them financially and with their prayers. Otherwise, *with no personal attention* many of these projects would have gone without adequate support.

Many hundreds of volunteers serving in Haiti have been powerfully affected by their experiences, perhaps as much or more than in most countries. This could be illustrated by a story concerning the building of a church center in a village called Petit-Goave. As a member of that team, I asked the pastor's wife if she could help me find the village of Bois Gency, where several teams from north Alabama, under the leadership of Ed Cowden, had built a church and were supporting the local Methodist school. She took me and a few team members over some rough terrain, including a dry river bed; then we got out and climbed about three miles up a mountain. After briefly visiting the school that was in session in the new Methodist Church building, we began our climb back down. On our way, we were startled to see a very ill little Haitian boy lying beside a tree, with hardly any clothes on and in enormous pain due to body swelling. His father was working his garden and came over to tell us the sad story of his wife's death, how he had spent all of his money on the child and could do nothing more for him, so he had brought his son here to die in the shade. All of us were shocked, and team member Mary Bass of Columbus, Georgia, asked what it would cost to admit the boy to the local hospital. It would be $20, a fortune for this good man. But Mary said, "I will gladly pay that charge." Now came the problem of how to get the child down the difficult mountain pass. Out from nowhere came the most beautiful mule I had ever seen! The wooden saddle on its back looked to be most uncomfortable until some of the Haitian women got cloths together to cushion it for the suffering child. The father took the reins and led the sick son and his older brother down the mountain pass. Mary said emphatically, "If this is what the work of mission is all about, you can count me in." Eventually, the boy recovered and was able to return to his home.

One of our faithful mission partners has been Bishop Alejandro Ruiz of the Methodist Church of Mexico. He said, "This movement is the best practical expression of mission concern because not just a few officials are involved, but ordinary local church members participate. I am fully convinced of its value to both the local church group here and those from outside."

Local people using their own initiative and creative talents are responding to the call of God through this avenue of Christian mission in amazing numbers all across our church. That is the genesis of the movement as it opens the door for service by all who are willing to offer.

I make no claim that this record is complete as to the history of the movement. What I have sought to do is follow the basic chronology of events known to me, which helped to shape this amazing development from the very grassroots of the church. The task has been a large one. I have often felt overwhelmed with the responsibility to convey the big picture in which so many have given so much of themselves to so many others.

Much of the book's focus is on the Southeast, where the movement was first officially organized on a jurisdictional basis. Our experiences as UMVIM coordinators were mostly from this part of the country. At the request of the General Board of Global Ministries, however, we solicited input from the other four jurisdictions for this record of volunteer mission service in The United Methodist Church. Both GBGM and the SEJ Administrative Council gave generous grants toward this project.

Hundreds of letters requesting information about early volunteer efforts were sent to churches and mission leaders across the country as we sought input from other conferences and jurisdictions, national missionaries, and overseas church leaders. I have tried to include most of those responses herein, given space limitations that also forced the elimination of the names of many strong leaders in the movement. To all those who have assisted with this project in any way, I offer my sincere thanks.

Excellent materials for input into this book were sent to me by many annual conferences, some contributions, of course, larger than others. Unfortunately, it was not possible to include all of that valuable information.

A number of references are made to UMVIM's ongoing relationship with the GBGM. My remarks on this subject have not been easy to make as so much has been at stake for both agencies, which were truly concerned for the right decisions to be made in this breaking of new ground. After the first one or two years, it became evident that we were going to face serious differences of opinion that could not be avoided. Therefore, my comments reflect that difficult time through which we have passed, which remains a part of the record. Mistakes have been made by all parties. It was easy for me to get caught up in the spontaneous enthusiasm of people going out for mission service so that at times I may not have been sufficiently aware of other considerations. I am sure too that it was difficult for the Global Ministries staff, accustomed to dealing with salaried missionary personnel, to adapt to the very different needs of volunteers over whom they would have no control.

I want to express my profound appreciation to so many who

have participated in the gathering of materials and preparation of this manuscript. First, to the UMVIM Board of Directors in the Southeastern Jurisdiction for officially sponsoring this project; to the Reverend Dr. Gordon Goodgame, Executive Secretary of the SEJ Administrative Council, and the Reverend John McCullough of the General Board of Global Ministries for generous grants to help with expenses in its production as a national record of mission ministries; to the five jurisdictional UMVIM offices, their colleagues in all the annual conferences, and to our partners in mission across the United States; to church colleagues in other lands, and especially to the multitude of volunteers themselves who have been the heart of this work.

This project of producing an account of the early development of the UMVIM movement was given to me as a challenge by our board of directors. Slowly mountains of material began to flow into my study at home. These came in response to my requests for input from participants and hosts around the world. It was obvious that as an aspiring writer I needed the assistance of a skilled editor.

Fortunately a missionary colleague from days in Zimbabwe, Skip Higgs of Nashville, recognized my plight and offered to help. In the process, she often referred to herself as one of our volunteers in mission. Having served as a career missionary who also strongly affirms the UMVIM concept of mission, Skip deserves special recognition as a member of the UMVIM family for her enormous contribution. All who love this movement are greatly indebted to her and to her gracious and supportive husband, Barnie, for their steadfast devotion to this cause so dear to the hearts of many of us.

I am particularly indebted to Dr. Michael C. Watson and the Reverend Dr. John T. Martin, Jr., not only for their devoted leadership of the UMVIM board for our nineteen years as coordinators but also for their enormous contributions to this history; to the late Reverend Larry Eisenberg for his reminders to me to "put pen to paper"; to Jeanne Page for her devoted service in transcribing the text from my tape recording in her usual dedicated manner as our longest serving staff member; to Bill and Melissa Gross, who served as consultants; to Dr. Douglas Newton for his support of our fund-raising efforts; to our daughter Cally, and to Dr. Jim and

Linda Fields for their editorial assistance. Last, I owe a debt I can never repay to my wife, Margaret, for all her support and encouragement over this long process, and to Cally, Tom Jr., and Julie, who always have been a source of inspiration to me through all my ministry.

I believe God has brought us to a new day in Christian mission. All United Methodists can rejoice in this spontaneous movement, which is catching fire all across our great church! We give thanks for its cumulative effect empowered by the Spirit of God. It is truly an amazing testimony to Christian love in action. Now, let me tell you the story of UMVIM and how it all came to pass.

CHAPTER ONE

Christian Love in Action

The Purpose and Scope of UMVIM

Breathe on me, Breath of God, fill me with life anew,
that I may love what thou dost love, and do what thou wouldst do.

Edwin Hatch, 1878 (John 20:22)

In the last three decades, a major historical development taking place in Christian mission has hardly been noticed by American church members. The movement has developed from the traditional idea of the full-time missionary to the concept of short-term volunteer service emphasizing laity involvement. This ongoing process had its more recent beginnings about thirty years ago, and continues to gain strength today. It is a huge paradigm shift in the way our church approaches mission—a new way of thinking.

To put this in historical perspective, let us go back to the beginning of mission work by the Methodist Church in the USA. In 1833, one of the first known American Methodist missionaries began service abroad. He was the Reverend Melville Cox of North Carolina, who went to Liberia practically on his own, without the backing of any board or mission society. Though he died of malaria only four months after his arrival in Liberia, he left behind a strong impulse for others to follow. The epitaph on his grave reads: "Though a thousand fall, let not Africa be given up." The century and a half after Melville Cox's death witnessed American missionaries by the thousands going all over the world, at a time when America was rising to political, economic, and military prominence. An unfortunate association of Christianity with American culture resulted, and its serious repercussions still exist today.

When Margaret and I went to Africa as young missionaries, it was with the idea of supporting the people there in their quest for self-determination. Upon arrival, we found other missionary colleagues had various other ideas about liberation from colonialism. Some still held old conservative beliefs and practices; they were the product of an earlier generation. Only a few years earlier, nationals and mission-aries had eaten in separate dining rooms at the annual conference. Many newer missionaries had more inclusive ideas about integration of the two groups, with an eye toward developing close teamwork.

This concern proved to be a constant struggle in the 1960s; but as time went on, more and more Africans went abroad to study, received their degrees, and came back home to assume leadership roles once held by missionaries. By the end of our last term in 1976, Africans were in key positions throughout the church. The number of missionaries had dwindled from a record high of about seventy in 1968 to fewer than a dozen. This marked a significant turning point for the church in Rhodesia (now Zimbabwe). Many other developing countries were experiencing similar revolutionary changes. Independence had come to Ghana in 1957 and then to the Belgian Congo in 1960. After that, dozens of countries in Africa, Asia, and the Caribbean pushed off colonial rule. Such political upheaval was having its impact on the churches, leading toward increased national leadership and away from missionary control.

To illustrate how this transition was working, in my last position as administrative assistant to Bishop Abel T. Muzorewa, I was succeeded by Dr. John W. Z. Kurewa, who later became head of Africa University. One of the first times that I remember preference being given to advancing African leadership was in the early sixties when James Makawa became head of Hartzell Teacher Training College at Old Mutare, replacing missionaries. Then Isaac Musamba succeeded missionary Reverend Robert Gates as conference treasurer. I remember that election well. The question at issue was whether the treasurer should be a layperson or a minister. Mr. Musamba, an outstanding layman who also served as conference layleader, was elected. A European (white Rhodesian) official at our local bank asked me how we could trust an African man with church funds. Mr. Musamba handled more than $1,000,000 a year quite efficiently, and his audit was always well received.

Perhaps the most significant sign of advancing national leadership in the church occurred in 1968 with the election of our denomination's first African bishop for Rhodesia. The Reverend Abel Tendekayi Muzorewa was elected that year to succeed retiring Bishop Ralph E. Dodge, who had led a major effort several years earlier to secure scholarships for some 150 students to American and British universities.

At the Africa Central Conference of 1968 (parallel to jurisdictional conferences in this country), I was elected general secretary and re-elected to that office in 1972. The Africa Central Conference of which Rhodesia was a part also included United Methodist conferences in Angola, Zaire, Zambia, Mozambique, and South Africa, involving several African tribal languages and the colonial languages French and Portuguese as well as English. Official discussions at central conference had to be translated for delegates who spoke English, French, or Portuguese as well as their own vernacular languages. My experiences in Central Conference gave me a much better understanding of our church's work continent-wide.

At that time, I was pastor of the Wesley United Methodist Church, an English-speaking congregation (meaning all-white at the time) in Rusape, a small town between Harare and Mutare. On the Sunday following central conference, I reported to the church my joy in the election of a "mwana wevu" (son of the soil) as our new bishop and said I would be looking forward to the time when he would be free to come and preach for us. This stirred up considerable consternation from some folk, but in a short while Bishop Muzorewa came to preach and was well received. I often felt my role at Rusape was one of reconciliation, a concept that I believe has always been crucial to ministry.

Many American Christians think missionaries are still in charge of much of the Christian work outside this country, which is quite false. I, for one, celebrate the coming of age of the United Methodist Church and sister Methodists worldwide, in which nationals take great pride and joy in being responsible for their own church's ministry. We now work in full partnership with nationals and always under their direction.

The Volunteers In Mission movement is an idea whose time has come. We have seen an easy and natural transition from the declining role of the traditional career missionary to the rapid growth of volunteer service in the mission program of the church. Easier transportation and communication have revolutionized the older forms of Christian mission. American churches now hear the story of the church in Africa and elsewhere far more often from volunteers than from career missionaries; and overseas churches are receiving many more short-term volunteers than career missionaries who normally expect to give longer periods of service with salary support. Even though today's volunteers serve shorter terms, their personal contacts and shared ministry are, from all accounts, exceedingly popular and productive with volunteers and host churches. Traditional missionaries will still be needed, especially in such places as the Muslim world where many years of study and living are required for effective ministry, or in other special circumstances. I think of today's volunteers as complementary to this long-established missionary tradition.

In Rhodesia we learned from experience how important it was for African people to feel that they, under God, were in control of their own destiny. It was central to their integrity as human beings; they wished to be recognized as the proper leadership of their church. The rise of the UMVIM movement at this particular time in history coincided with this determination of national Christians in Rhodesia to take charge of their own affairs, while they were eager and ready to receive volunteers who would serve among them and under their direction. This same lesson has carried over in relations with colleague churches and leaders of volunteers in mission in many other lands around the globe.

In addition to the shift away from dominant missionary leadership, the volunteers in mission movement came along in response to increasing interest by the laity and clergy in the USA to have hands-on mission experience, at the invitation of national church leaders who had expressed a need for help. In 1976, when UMVIM was established as an official organized movement in the Southeast, no other office of coordination existed in the United Methodist Church. Virtually all mission programs were served by trained career missionaries and administered by the World Division or National Division of the General Board of Global Ministries. Helping the mission board to recognize the new reality in mission was not an easy task. I could understand the board's hesitation up to a point, for in my early days with UMVIM I had many of the same reservations. Mission board staff worked with a more settled group of salaried career missionaries, not volunteers who came and went frequently. Board staff could not adequately appreciate the volunteers' enthusiasm and commitment. Some felt that volunteers could be more hindrance than help.

During this period, the volunteers in mission movement had to be persistent in its struggle for official recognition, which finally came at the 1980 General Conference. The change by mission officials has come gradually with much dialogue, disagreement, and tension. In the past few years, however, GBGM officials and UMVIM leaders have reached a mutual understanding that speaks well for the future.

The UMVIM approach has always been to seek the approval and guidance of overseas national leaders or mission agencies in the United States. I came to embrace this concept during my years of working with African colleagues and supporting their leadership roles. The building and maintenance of such relationships is very sensitive and extremely important. Our cardinal rule of operation has been to seek an invitation from a host mission group before proceeding in any situation. This policy has meant much travel for the UMVIM director and others, visiting in the countries of the overseas church leaders, conferring with them about the purpose of the volunteer ministry and laying the foundation for ongoing personal relationships, which form the cornerstone of our work. The genuine welcoming spirit that I found was greatly encouraging.

UMVIM teams go out in a cooperative spirit, offering what we have in materials and personnel to a local conference or community. We go to meet and get to know our sisters and brothers in Christ, to help each other as we can to strengthen the ministries of the local churches, and to share with one another our experience of what it means to be a Christian living in today's world. In turn, we receive new understanding of faith and of God's work among the poor and disenfranchised. Our hosts' contagious spirit and love of Christ have a great impact on the lives of all volunteers. The experience for us all is indeed one of true mutuality in mission.

I have visited most countries where UMVIM volunteers have served. My first step in a new country was to contact the bishop or other head of the church—usually a United Methodist, Methodist-related, or ecumenical group—to ask if I could come for a visit. The response was invariably, "Yes, when can you come?" As I shared with the bishops or other church leaders our desire to work only with designated church leaders on a project or program in some area of need, they were usually surprised. Many groups from the USA have gone abroad without clearing their plans with national leaders, determining for themselves where and how they would work. Such plans may or may not be made with a local Methodist pastor. In addition, independent mission groups in the USA using United Methodist members may set up their own contacts, often apart from local Methodist officials. This procedure may result from a friendship with an overseas pastor who sees an opportunity to do something good for his or her church without consulting local church officials. Although born of the best intentions, such individual plans, if encouraged, create unnecessary tension in the church and a sense of competition for outside support. Such independent service seems to be declining as more United Methodists learn there is a proper and effective channel through UMVIM by which they can receive guidance and placement for a hands-on mission experience in a spirit of mutual respect.

UMVIM's dedication to correct procedure with respect to our hosts anywhere in the world can be seen in a visit that a former UMCOR staff member and I made to the island of Dominica in 1977 to discuss relief work following a devastating hurricane. We met with the Reverend Donald Henry, president of the Methodist Church in the Caribbean and the Americas (MCCA), who made it clear that our work must be under the direction of the local Methodist pastors. We assured him that was the way we intended to work. This visit proved to be a strong, positive experience, helping to open the door to future ministries with the entire MCCA.

Later that same year I made my first extensive visit across the Caribbean with the Reverend Joseph Perez of the General Board of Global Ministries. We met personally with a number of the key leaders with whom UMVIM would be working on a regular basis. I quickly understood that personal contacts would be crucial to the success of UMVIM's future in the Caribbean and Central America, where much of its work has taken place.

As we witness the decreasing role of traditional missionaries, the volunteers in mission movement is rising from the grassroots as a complementary avenue of service. I earnestly believe that this missional thrust was raised up by God at this time to work with church leaders here and in other countries. UMVIM respects the need of overseas churches to be independent, while also providing a new avenue of ministry for dedicated Christians who want to reach out to people and churches in crisis with their skills and talents.

My own change of heart, as I like to call it, came after nearly two years of observing and studying the movement. Given my background of service in Rhodesia where advancement of national church leaders was a major concern, it had been difficult for me to see why so many American Christians felt a call for short-term experience as volunteers. I had to struggle as GBGM officials did, but I was much closer to the scene and eventually could see the exciting potential of this movement.

Two things impressed me strongly in my second year as coordinator. First was the warm welcome I received in visits to overseas and home-mission project leaders. They were keen to invite volunteers to come if they had been well trained for their job and observed proper protocol. Second was the excitement and joy in the faces of volunteers as they returned home and gave their reports. Here was clear evidence of changed lives with a deeper appreciation for the work of the church around the world, with a new awareness of the global church and its complexities, and a greater knowledge and interest in the church's total mission program. There was no way to deny these facts.

Thus it was that I began to experience much joy in helping to work out placements for teams and individuals, all eager to serve on a first-hand basis. Often in the office I was called upon to help some church group locate a place where it could serve. What a great opportunity this presented for me to work directly in matching people to a project and helping them grow in the process. Offers of service began to increase dramatically from all over the country. Many individuals and teams were asking for help in placement and preparation.

For example, Sally Bevill Del Castillo of Mississippi came to the office in Atlanta to tell me of her strong interest in going to a Latin American country for the months of April, May, and June, when she would be free from her work. Since volunteers take full financial responsibility for all their personal expense, and she was able to do that and had asked for our assistance with placement, I felt the way was clear. A request had recently come from Bishop Eugenio Poma of Bolivia for some volunteers to help pastors and layleaders improve their English. Sally and I joked together about our southern English, as we are both southerners, and wondered if she would be understood. After completing the training course, Sally began her mission journey. She had been in Bolivia for a few weeks when Bishop Poma called one day to say how glad he was that she had come. He said, "We just 'luv' Sally! Can you send us another Sally?" How much clearer picture could be painted of the impact of this personal form of mission?

One of the most exciting teams with which I have worked was from Bethel and Ben Hill, two predominantly African American United Methodist churches in Atlanta. Our story with them began in 1991 when they asked my help in planning an overseas mission. I immediately suggested Zimbabwe, thinking this would have special appeal. They gave us an enthusiastic response.

It was a high privilege to be present with them for a service of worship and dedication at Bethel Church a few weeks before the team left for Africa. Fortunately Zimbabwe's Bishop Christopher Jokomo was in the USA at that time and had come to preach at Bethel Church on this special occasion. When the team members embarked on their journey, Margaret and I went to see them off at the airport. Their excitement could hardly be contained.

Upon their arrival in Harare, Zimbabwe's capital, the group went by bus for the final leg of their journey to Nyamuzuwe High School, where Barnie and Skip Higgs were pioneers. Until the school was founded in 1958, children in the area had little hope of an education beyond Standard Four (sixth grade). Nyamuzuwe is in a remote area about one hundred miles from Harare. Unfortunately, the team's bus broke down at about eight o'clock that night, and they were isolated on a lonely stretch of gravel road until nearly midnight when the Mtoko district superintendent came along. He said he was looking for a team of American volunteers, not thinking that this busload of people would be the group he sought! After his initial surprise, he quickly arranged alternative transportation to Nyamuzuwe and the team's first night's sleep on African soil. This was the first African American international UMVIM team to be organized through our office. An earlier all-black mission team from Bethune-Cookman College in Florida had served in Haiti.

The group received a wonderful welcome at Nyamuzuwe by the local people. Their assigned task was to paint a dormitory built in honor of Mildred Taylor, a longtime missionary to Zimbabwe from the North Alabama Conference. This they did and much more. They have talked about how much it meant to them to have close contacts with students and faculty, and to share experiences and faith.

Before the team left Zimbabwe, they went to Old Mutare to visit Africa University. Since returning home, they have been busy telling the story of church work and the new university in Zimbabwe with great excitement. It is encouraging to see teams that are truly representative of our church's racial and intercultural makeup. Many teams come from predominately white congregations and often are limited to a mainly white composition, which is surely understandable up to a point. Our hosts often comment about the fact that the complexion of team members does not seem to represent the diversity of our churches. Many organizing groups work hard to be inclusive in the membership of their teams.

UMVIM's outreach was stretching farther and farther around the globe. In South Carolina, the Reverend Jim Mishoe was preparing a series of teams to go to the Philippines to help develop a major church center there. Others from south Georgia and elsewhere joined in this effort, which had the strong backing of the bishop and other leaders in Manila. Eventually the Methodist Church in the Philippines developed its own Volunteers In Mission movement across the country and in adjacent areas. Teams were also going to work with the Methodist Church in Southern Africa, which has now formed its own Southern Africa Methodist Volunteers In Mission ministry (SAMVIM), patterned largely on the UMVIM model. A ministry of this same type is developing in Zimbabwe. And in the 1990s, UMVIM teams and individual volunteers have gone out to hundreds of United States mission projects and disaster relief efforts across the country, including burned churches, and to every continent.

The Great Commission has been heard and taken seriously by many volunteers who have found an avenue through the UMVIM movement to use their talents and skills in practical ways to carry out its mandate.

CHAPTER TWO

On a Wing and a Prayer
The UMVIM Pioneers

Every valley shall be exalted and every mountain and hill shall be made low: and the crooked shall be made straight, and the rough places plain.

Isaiah 40:4 (KJV)

The UMVIM movement began with a number of strong, committed Christians at the grassroots level of the church who had a great desire to serve God through the personal use of their talents and energies. They were already involved in local church and community service projects, but had become increasingly concerned about urgent needs beyond their local communities, even in overseas areas. They wanted to do something to help. Here and there, individuals and groups began to organize themselves around projects they identified. Their excitement was contagious and quickly spread to others. I interviewed some of the early pioneers and caught their spirit as they described the growing framework that would mold the future of the UMVIM movement.

One of the principal pioneers and founding fathers of the movement in the Southeast is Dr. Michael C. Watson of Bamberg, South Carolina. Mike, as he is affectionately known by many coworkers, is a busy family physician, county medical officer, and active United Methodist at all levels of the church. He and the Reverend George Strait, pastor of a nearby United Methodist church, were fast friends in the 1950s and 1960s, sharing a deep love of mission and a common concern that the missionary task had become too impersonal with its major emphasis on fundraising. Mike said of that period:

It seemed to us that our national Board of Missions was not taking advantage of the age of the jet airplane in sending out missionaries only for extended periods of time. We thought surely the mission field could use the multiple talents of the rest of us for shorter terms of service that were available for the asking. Equally important, if not more so, opportunities to volunteer would provide an avenue for more meaningful participation in the life of the church for many laypersons.

George was a pharmacist before going to seminary. We both felt that to prove our point we would start with physicians who could more likely afford the cost of an overseas trip, as our program had no funds. We did not envision a purely overseas program, but felt we should start there as it would attract more attention at the beginning. Then as things developed, we would include a thrust for mission outreach at home and even in our own neighborhoods.

We discussed this many times and decided to enlighten the General Board of Missions with our inspiration. We wrote the board and told them of our ideas but received no reply. In our own South Carolina Conference, we got busy and promoted the idea of volunteerism, resulting in the Summer Investment Program, which challenged selected college students to a summer of mission activity. The Reverend David Reese, through his strong leadership, enabled our conference to lead the jurisdiction in mission giving that year.

Not long after this, Reese invited George and me to go with him to a mission fair in Charlotte at the Myers Park Church. The focus was on a medical team that had recently returned from a mission to South America. George and I were ecstatic to learn that what we had been dreaming about was actually happening, but from a local church base.

On the way home, the three of us continued talking enthusiastically. We were filled with admiration for the mission team that had taken more than thirty persons of various medical specialties into a remote area of Bolivia for about two weeks. I came to feel that short-term volunteers could best be used to reinforce an existing facility, not to start a mission ministry, which might raise all kinds of hopes and expectations that could be dashed two weeks later. We became more convinced that a structure of some kind, such as UMVIM eventually became, was needed to offer training and guidance to this movement so that each first-time effort would not be doomed to repeat mistakes that had been made over and over by others. And we had always been convinced that such a program should be firmly housed within the General Board of Missions. After this, we heard of several other programs of volunteer activity, but always with a local church base.

Over the next few years, Watson's experience in the church was increasingly recognized, and he was chosen as one of our denomination's representatives to the National Council of Churches, a member of the Methodist Committee on Relief, and later as a member of the newly organized General Board of Global Ministries. All of this helped prepare him for a major role in the development of the UMVIM ministry.

Then a significant breakthrough came. "In the fall of 1968," Mike recalled:

I had an unexpected call from Dr. James Thomas, a staff member of the United Methodist Committee on Relief. He told me of Aguilla, a little island in the southern Caribbean that would be losing its only doctor that coming January. Thomas said, "I have heard so much from you about your South Carolina doctors and what they can do. Why don't you go down there and see if you can help out?" I immediately answered yes and arranged to be on my way in two days. I hung up the phone with mixed emotions. I was a little panicky at the idea of getting ready in such a short time, and even more at being away from home and practice. In another way, I was in seventh heaven. After fourteen years, we at last had a mission challenge. I could hardly wait to tell George!

This exciting development for Mike led him "to spread the word to anyone who would listen in the various national meetings I attended. Most listened politely but gave no indication that the volunteer movement would ever penetrate the general church structure. A number of meetings in which I was involved were held from time to time and the idea was discussed, but still no action."

Determined not to rush ahead, Mike was nonetheless keen that this challenge be pursued. He reported:

During this period of intense canvassing for support of the ministry, I found that Dr. Harry Haines, chief executive of UMCOR, and I disagreed on only one thing. That was my belief in an urgent need to establish an office of coordination as part of Global Ministries, which Harry opposed. Although UMCOR made extensive use of volunteers in relief teams, Harry felt that volunteerism would lose its spontaneity and be smothered as a structured program of the church. On the other hand, I maintained that if we were going to be authentic and available to the entire connection, we had to be in the structure somewhere. I remember once I had an opportunity with Dr. John Schaeffer, then head of the World Division, to discuss this issue. Harry followed me almost up to Schaeffer's door arguing against it. Unfortunately, that discussion with Schaeffer produced no results.

Opportunities continued to come to Dr. Watson through UMCOR: a landslide in Honduras following a hurricane, an earthquake in Nicaragua, a severe hurricane in Dominica, and more. Volunteers rose to each occasion in a very fine way. Another opportunity came through a meeting in Miami in 1966 with the Reverend J. Lloyd Knox, then district superintendent and later bishop. He opened the way for contact in Nicaragua with Dr. Gustavo Parajon, who was coordinating the use of medical volunteers in two Moravian hospitals on the east coast of Nicaragua. Toward the end of 1972, Managua suffered a severe earthquake. "I went down with my fourteen-year-old son, Mike, Jr., and met with Dr. Parajon. Thus began a long line of volunteer physicians, nurses, medical technologists, and others into that country."

Mike's stories continue:

Once when I was speaking at a Global Ministries meeting in Chicago about our volunteer service, the Reverend Dwight Busacca of the North Central Jurisdiction mission office was present. Later that day on a flight, he talked to his seatmate, Dr. J. Preston Hughes, a surgeon from New Orleans, about the plight in Nicaragua and gave him my name. I received a ham-radio distress call from Nicaragua that the only surgeon in the region had been confined to bed, so no surgeon was available to the entire eastern half of the country. Dr. Hughes called, expressed interest in serving, and went. He wrote later, "Dr. Watson, I have had the most memorable several weeks of my life. While I was there, one of the nurses had a ruptured ectopic pregnancy and would have died if I had not been there to operate." During this time and for the next ten years or so as my interest in using volunteers became widely known in our church, a great many of the requests for volunteer medical service coming to Global Ministries were channeled to me for disposition and assignment.

One nonmedical mission was created after a hurricane in Dominica where winds of over two hundred miles per hour pounded the island for over twenty-four hours. I had not seen such destruction as this since World War II, when I served as a private first class with the U.S. Marine Corps in the Pacific and saw massive destruction from preinvasion naval sea and air bombardment. Many homes had their roofs blown off, so we sent a number of construction teams to help with their replacement.

Thus it was that these two Christians, Mike Watson and George Strait, one a layman and the other clergy, provided the ongoing impetus in the very early years, which would lead eventually to the organized movement that came to be known as United Methodist Volunteers In Mission. Similar leadership was being shown in other conferences such as Western North Carolina, under the direction of the Reverend Bill Bobbitt and the Reverend Joel Key. In the Florida Conference, the same development was taking place through the leadership of the Reverend H. W. Parker and the Reverend Delmas Copeland. In the Holston Conference, the Reverend John Trundle was the pioneer and driving force. In the North Georgia Conference two laymen took the lead, William Kagebein and Kenneth Vining. Elsewhere across the country, others were also seeking to establish such a movement in their own areas.

It was soon evident that the rapid growth in volunteer involvement at the grassroots necessitated the creation of an office of coordination to guide its development. Mike Watson had seen the need quite early, and leadership for the office was to come about within the next year on a part-time basis.

The Reverend Bill Starnes played a pivotal role at this developmental stage. He had been a missionary to Zaire and was then Southeastern field representative for the General Board of Global Ministries. Bill had witnessed a groundswell of personal interest in hands-on mission involvement throughout the SEJ and was eager for it to be on a more secure footing. Believing this to be "the wave of the future" (his words), he called for a meeting of interested persons on June 8, 1974, in Atlanta and arranged for the Reverend Randle Dew, head of the National Division's volunteer program, to come as a representative from Global Ministries.

"About thirty-five people came, and most of us did not know each other," Mike recalled. "We were delighted to learn of each other's work with volunteers. I remember several people who were there and with whom I began long relationships in the movement, as well as personal friendships. All were key leaders in developing the office of coordination, and their support and encouragement were indispensable in these early months and years."

Dr. Watson recalled, "When we began to plan for the future of the volunteer movement and its goal to do extensive mission work at home and overseas, Randy Dew, mission board representative, said, 'You can't do that,' citing the disciplinary requirement of obtaining permission from the GBGM prior to overseas mission involvement. Someone said in return, 'We didn't ask you if we could do it, because we are going to do it. The question is, will you help us?' Dew could not answer this, so the group continued planning."

Attention now turned to developing an ad hoc Steering Committee that would be responsible for guiding the work of volunteers in the Southeastern Jurisdiction. This group recommended that the steering committee serve in an advisory and facilitating capacity rather than taking over the basic responsibility; that it only encourage churches to respond on specific projects if they were paying their full share of World Service and conference benevolence asking; and that it must not act to control or suppress the grassroots nature of the movement.

Such an attitude on the part of the Steering Committee demonstrated its vision and concern that volunteer mission projects not be considered a way of avoiding other mission responsibilities. It also clearly showed an understanding that ownership of the volunteer movement was at the grassroots level of the church.

Dr. Watson continued:

The outcome of this meeting was that we felt our best avenue would be to organize a jurisdictional structure that would suit our needs for furthering the cause of volunteerism in our denomination. We agreed to ask Global Ministries for support and assigned Bill Starnes and me the task of negotiating with them. Bill Starnes suggested that the board assign another person to his office, whose time would be divided between promoting the Advance [official mission funding program] and supporting an office for volunteers.

Correspondence flowed rather freely among mission board staff members during this period of negotiation. Dr. Watson was the primary SEJ representative at this critical stage of development. The board staff seemed eager to ensure that their normal guidelines with regard to international mission were being followed without sufficiently understanding the dynamics of the volunteer movement. They were applying the same principles to volunteers as to traditional missionaries, yet the two forms of mission service were quite different.

A letter from the SEJ Steering Committee secretary, the Reverend John Trundle, to a GBGM staff member illustrates the gap existing at that time between the Board of Global Ministries and the Steering Committee: "It does not matter to us whether we get cooperation from New York or not. We made the initial overture and opened the door. We feel that what we are doing is worthwhile, but it does not seem to us at this point that there is any flexibility in New York." One of the key issues was how churches supporting Volunteers In Mission could properly receive Advance mission credit, instead of simply being credited as a local benevolence. The point of contention was that to receive Advance mission credit would have assumed the board's approval of the volunteer activity, an approval that was still several years away.

The Steering Committee held a consultation in Atlanta on March 26, 1974, with Global Ministries representatives and about thirty other persons. A further meeting that July at Lake Junaluska led to an official approach to the GBGM for a missionary couple to serve as coordinators. Broad outlines were drawn up for this future work.

At the July meeting, a statement of important operation principles was adopted, which emphasized that the initiative for a work team project would come from the field and that volunteers would work in cooperation with local leadership. Stress was given to maximum honesty and sensitivity in all relationships; no local church would participate unless it had met its other mission obligations. Volunteers would be screened, trained, and available for interpretation upon return home. Teams would be broadly representative with regard to racial composition. Work would be done *with* people, not *for* them.

These early signs of responsible leadership on the part of the Steering Committee are certainly to be commended. Their vision was, first, to ensure that mission work be in a true spirit of mutuality and with proper respect for the role of volunteer ministries in the general life of the host church. The committee also began to give attention to organizing and developing conference volunteers in mission committees, though some were already at work. Investigation into new mission opportunities was also moving into high gear.

The initial UMVIM Steering Committee was officially organized in 1975 and chaired by Dr. George Holmes of Western North Carolina Conference. When Dr. Holmes resigned for reasons of health in 1976, Mike Watson took over as chair of that important committee and continued until 1988.

Dr. Watson added, "After our negotiations, the GBGM assigned the Reverend David and Dr. Mary Sue Lowry as the first coordinators to assist us on a part-time basis and provided full missionary support for them for one year. The Lowrys had been serving in Chile and were home on furlough. Their assignment, which began early in 1974, was to spend the majority of their time on mission interpretation. They were a godsend to us at that time, giving invaluable service by helping to bring a scattered movement together and give it substance."

According to Dr. Watson, "The Lowrys had left Chile in body, but their hearts were still there; and as soon as they could, in less than a year, the couple returned to Chile. The Office of Coordination opened for business for the first time in August 1975, just before David left for Chile in September. Mary Sue followed a few months later. After the Lowrys' return to Chile, the office was vacant for almost a year."

I asked David and Mary Sue Lowry to reflect on their assignment as the first coordinators. His response indicated their concern that the board seemed reluctant to join in wholeheartedly with the movement. He said, "Our contacts with persons from the Southeast convinced us that they were on fire for the concept and were nearly to the point of saying they were ready to go ahead, with or without the help of the World Division. Mary Sue and I felt strongly that if the World Division wished to have any input at all, this was the place to begin that cooperation and the time to do it."

CHAPTER THREE

New Coordinators on Board

Be anxious for nothing, but in everything by prayer and supplication, with thanksgiving, let your requests be made known to God; and the peace of God, which surpasses all understanding, will guard your hearts and minds through Christ Jesus.

Philippians 4:6, 7 (NKJV)

Global Ministries' staff and SEJ representatives met late in 1975 to discuss a replacement for the Lowrys, who were due to return to Chile that year. Mike Watson recalled:

On August 19, 1975, Dr. Holmes, Needham Williamson, and I met with representatives of the various divisions of the board. While we found the group to be interested and helpful, we were given no absolute assurance of continuing help from them. We were asked to submit a proposal with evaluations, and the staff would carry our concerns to appropriate agencies within the board. This style of operation continued as the board formed an Interdivisional Task Force to relate to us. We met with the task force on a periodic basis in New York and submitted our bylaws, evaluations, and job description for use by the new coordinators. This arrangement continued even into the first years with our second coordinators, Tom and Margaret Curtis, who were then serving as missionaries in Rhodesia.

Margaret and I had received an invitation from Dr. Isaac Bivens, then head of the Africa office of the GBGM, in January 1976 while we were still in Africa, asking if we would consider accepting this position upon our arrival home that year. At that point we were feeling the need to have our family together in one place for a while as Carolyn, our oldest child, was already in college in the USA, Tom Jr. was in high school and facing a likely draft into the Rhodesian army within a few months, and Julie, our youngest, was still in grade school. The idea of working from our home for a year or two sounded like an ideal plan for us. We were pleased to accept the invitation.

In February 1976 the mission-board staff reviewed the work of David and Mary Sue Lowry as they were preparing to return to Chile and confirmed the invitation to Margaret and me to assume the position of coordinators for the Southeastern Jurisdiction as of June 1. I first met with the newly established GBGM Interdivisional VIM Task Force the next month in New York. The purpose of our meeting was to consider our role, the task force's guidelines for work, personal expectations, and financial arrangements for the Office of Coordination. Our assignment was to give approximately half time to mission interpretation and the other half to the coordination of volunteers.

We began a heavy schedule of speaking engagements across the country, as Rhodesia was very much in the news. This also gave me a chance to gradually get acquainted with the UMVIM movement. My purpose then was to find out what was driving the desire of people to participate so eagerly in volunteerism and to learn as much as possible about the movement.

I do not know any specific reason why we were selected to be given this opportunity, except perhaps that we would be back for furlough within the year and that we were from the Southeast, and Atlanta would be a convenient place for us to live. I later understood that the board was seeking a couple with extensive experience outside this country. We had earnestly tried to have a close personal working relationship with national colleagues in Africa, and I like to think that would have been a factor in our selection.

As for Margaret and me, our perspective on mission service comes from a number of years as traditional missionaries on the African continent in a dynamic and growing church. We had many learning experiences in Africa that helped prepare us for future service with UMVIM. At this point, I would like to give some of our background in mission service.

Our missionary careers, in a sense, go back to the time of our calling to mission. In Margaret's case, this calling began when she was a teenager, through the influence of her home Methodist church in Clay, Alabama. My commitment was made while a student at Asbury College in 1949, though my initial interest had begun earlier as a young member of First Methodist Church in Albany, Georgia.

After our marriage in 1953 this interest continued through two-and-one-half years of home-mission service with the Salvation Army in West Virginia and Maryland. Our commitment was maintained during seminary days at the Candler School of Theology, where I obtained my master of divinity degree, and through two-and-one-half years as a student pastor. We were accepted for service by the Methodist Board of Missions upon graduation in 1958, but felt led to accept an invitation from Dr. Frank Robertson for me to serve two years as associate pastor at St. Luke Methodist Church in Columbus, Georgia. He was keen that St. Luke develop a strong personal tie with our family, which might result in a significant involvement in our future mission ministry and in general missionary support by the congregation. This was indeed providential, as St. Luke became one of our most faithful supporting churches and remained so for more than forty years.

In June 1960 we were commissioned as missionaries of the Methodist Church by Bishop Arthur J. Moore at Atlanta's First Methodist Church during a session of the North Georgia Conference, just prior to Bishop Moore's retirement.

On September 1, 1960, Margaret and I, along with six-year-old Carolyn and one-year-old Tommy, set sail for England to continue our missionary training for four months at Selly Oak Colleges in Birmingham. This ecumenical center was established by a number of churches, including the British Methodist Conference, to prepare persons for mission service throughout the world.

At the Selly Oak libraries we found generous supplies of material on the British colony of Southern Rhodesia (now Zimbabwe) to which we had been assigned by the Board of Missions. This was important information for us, as we would soon be immersed in an entirely new way of living and working as "permanent residents" in a colonial system of government.

We also were blessed at Selly Oak with the presence of a fine faculty that cared for its students, as well as rich fellowship with experienced missionaries and those going out for the first time. I think one of the greatest advantages, however, was becoming accustomed to British customs and culture, which would be a strong influence on our lives for many years in Africa.

In January 1961 we arrived in Southern Rhodesia and began language training at Nyakatsapa, a rural church and school center related to the Southern Rhodesia Annual Conference. This was where we first encountered living and working in a language entirely different from English and began to acquire some understanding of the Shona culture. This effort continued during our sixteen years of service in that country.

At first we were overwhelmed with the enormous differences in lifestyle. This period of transition and adaptation takes time, but fortunately we felt that the strong support of our colleagues—nationals and missionaries—greatly facilitated necessary changes in our daily pattern of living. One has only to consider what this means in terms of a family with two small children—adjusting to buying food, preparing meals, caring for the household, becoming involved in one's own mission service—to realize that adapting to a new culture does not come easily or quickly or without mistakes. We found the African people were most gracious in overlooking our slow learning in many circumstances. We can readily identify with the short-term volunteers who are frustrated by puzzling customs and quite different lifestyles.

One of the first and most important changes came in realizing that we are all God's children, regardless of race or national background. As one who grew up in the segregated South, I was a product of that time, but was not conscious of any prejudice. I must hasten to say, however, that my close work with African pastors and laypeople as a district superintendent soon helped me to overcome any misgiving I may have had. On a number of occasions, pastors risked their lives for me. Several times while traveling out in the bush (rural areas), I was told to remain inside one of their homes as it was not safe to be outside.

One Saturday night I had a strange feeling when all was very quiet and none of the usual singing or laughter could be heard around the campfire. I had been shown where I would sleep, in a small rondavel (round hut). After I went to bed, several men came in to sleep beside me on both sides. The next morning the district layleader and I left the site around five o'clock. When we had gone quite a distance, he said we had left trouble behind. Two nights before, a gang of African youths had come through and killed the chief, whom they considered a "sell-out" to the white colonial government. The pastor feared that the gang might return, and seeing me, a white man, could cause trouble. So they hastened me away.

There is no way I can express my joy of fellowship with so many African friends and the impact they have made on my life. I will never be the same. But bonding takes time and a willingness to be open and to learn.

For the Shona people of Zimbabwe, people and their traditions are of the utmost value. The Shona people may match the Japanese in politeness and gentility in the rituals of daily life. I could illustrate this with many incidents. For example, an African layman and I were expected out in the district for an appointment with a group of people. Just as we were about to leave my house, an elderly African woman arrived. She had walked several miles to see me as her district superintendent. I knew it would take time to visit with her properly, and then we would be late for our appointment. But I decided to invite her into the house, Margaret served her tea as is the custom, and we exchanged greetings. This took at least half an hour. Finally we got down to talking about the business on her mind. When we bade her farewell and were on our journey, the layman said to me, "Tom, I was watching to see if you would take time with that woman or rush on to the appointment. You did the right thing. We think it's best to give attention to the person at hand, rather than in the distance." I thanked him and asked him please to feel free always to advise me in such cases. In fact, I often told friends, even begged them, to share freely with me. It is so easy to go out on a limb unnecessarily for failing to learn from others.

People are always important, but time is another factor to be considered. For most Americans, time is of the essence. Not so with many other peoples, who see time from an entirely different perspective. In Africa, for example, a worship service may be scheduled to begin at a time designated by pointing to the horizon at a certain level, which could mean almost any hour! One grows accustomed to services lasting two or more hours. One gets into the rhythm of the service and enjoys it, or else becomes miserable.

Learning to understand the importance of education in many African countries was another invaluable experience. One of my assignments was as principal of Nyamuzuwe Methodist High School, in a remote rural area one hundred miles from the capital city. The people were greatly disadvantaged due to poor soil and lack of rain. Even so, they sacrificed greatly in order to pay school fees for their children to stay in school. I will never forget these parents' strong commitments, despite great difficulties. Most students at Nyamuzuwe were on work scholarships. At this small mission boarding school in the sun-drenched sands of Mtoko district, with villages all around where subsistence farming was the way of life, I first understood that education truly held the key to a better future for the next generation. This sense of the importance of education in their lives made a profound impression on me. This same thirst for education is witnessed by volunteers wherever they go.

Wherever we were appointed to live, Margaret worked with the women of the church as a member of the Rukwadzano Rwe Wadzimai (Fellowship of Women), a powerful organization in the church, family, and community. She participated in many RRW events and gained insight into African family life and values. Most of her work was in leadership training. At Old Mutare, she taught Bible classes for the wives of students at the Biblical Institute and home craft classes in the village nearby. While we lived in Harare, she organized classes for teenage girls who had no opportunity for a regular high-school education, realizing that the potential these young women had would be diminished unless the church could help them. She taught English classes at Epworth Theological College for the students' wives who wanted to improve their communication skills. Valuable insights gained with the strong church women of Rhodesia have remained with her as a positive influence.

Serving in Rusape as pastor of Wesley United Methodist Church, our denomination's only English-speaking congregation in the country at that time, had a strong impact on my spiritual perspective. Here was a basically segregated community dominated by whites with an attitude somewhat benevolent at best toward the black majority. At our first meeting with the church official board, I was told that the church was for whites only. When my turn came to respond, I cited the *Discipline* of our church, which declares the doors open to all. Over the next four years, we maintained an open-door policy and preached respect and dignity for all people.

Out of the Rusape appointment grew important contacts with government leaders. The contacts with Europeans (whites) eventually led to my being called upon by Prime Minister Ian Smith to help initiate discussions with my own Bishop Abel Muzorewa. Smith was considered the most powerful white leader of the time, and Muzorewa the most powerful black. Knowledge gained from these negotiations was profound and had a great impact on my ministry. It opened doors for my involvement in the self-determination of the African majority. Being a full-time traditional missionary has the advantage of building relationships based on trust over a long period of time. Short-term volunteers are limited in this respect, but many long-term friendships develop, which may lead to positive social reform. This is especially true when volunteers return repeatedly to a given area of service.

Through all the political and social struggles, it was quite natural that my Christian faith would be tested and stretched. I came to see in the clearest terms the wholeness of the gospel, that there could be no separation into "personal" and "social," for it is all one gospel. An African friend who was a pastor said once that he had "never met a soul that did not have a body!" My traditional evangelical background would mature and deepen with this larger view of the gospel. I was learning from the people I had come to serve! In the midst of pain, the people with whom we served often responded with a resilience and gracious spirit that enabled them to overcome difficulties and limitations and keep going on. We quickly learned to appreciate and support such people and to remain open to new insights, which came almost daily.

A wide variety of cultural differences became evident after a while, including the different ways of interpreting our Christian faith. All of this can mean a tremendous growth in understanding if one's mind is open to truth. Lessons learned from these experiences in Africa were invaluable to Margaret and me as we sought to provide guidance to the growing UMVIM movement. Life among the Mashona helped us to know first-hand many of the problems that might emerge in service as volunteers.

After our years in Africa, Margaret and I immediately set up an office for UMVIM at our home. The 1976 SEJ Conference officially established our positions as coordinators and placed us within the jurisdictional structure. This was significant as the Steering Committee was eager to work through official channels. Previously, the work had been done by an ad hoc committee with Global Ministries' cooperation. We started our work in a spare room in our apartment, with the understanding that our time would be divided roughly between mission interpretation and coordination of the movement. Global Ministries fully covered our salary as missionaries on furlough for the first three years. That was a major contribution on their part and helped to ensure the continuation of the ministry at its beginning. After the three-year period had passed, again the board came through with annual grants on a decreasing scale, which helped enormously in the transition period to full responsibility being assumed by the Southeastern Jurisdiction in 1979 for staff salary and all office expenses.

In the following paragraphs, Dr. Michael Watson tells how the movement came to be officially adopted as a mission ministry in the Southeast, just when our appointment as coordinators was being finalized. "In 1976," Mike Watson says:

I was a delegate to the SE Jurisdictional Conference and happened to sit by Dr. Gordon Goodgame, a pastor and mission leader from the Holston Conference. In our discussion, Gordon said, "If you want the volunteer movement tied to the jurisdiction, you will have to have it done at this meeting or wait another four years." I asked how this could be done. He suggested that we ask to come under the umbrella of the jurisdiction's Fellowship of Conference Mission Secretaries (FCMS), and said I would have to introduce a resolution to that effect. The time for submitting resolutions in the regular way had long since passed, but if a subject was brought up during the conference session, a resolution could be submitted on that subject. Our volunteer efforts were mentioned by a representative of the College of Bishops in his State of the Jurisdiction Address, so the way was clear. I introduced a resolution that passed without discussion, and we officially became a part of the jurisdictional structure.

In my haste, I had not consulted with the FCMS about such a move, so I attended their first meeting during the conference, at which I said, "I feel like an orphan who has succeeded in adopting himself into a family without their knowledge or consent." My fears were groundless, as the fellowship accepted us in good grace and with considerable enthusiasm and have supported us strongly over the years.

At that joint meeting of the steering committee and the FCMS, we obtained permission for our corresponding secretary to write each of the district mission secretaries requesting an annual contribution of $50 per district for support of the new office.

This effort through the districts became one of the chief means of support for the Office of Coordination for volunteer mission teams, with some districts giving much larger amounts than requested. But increasingly the financial burden was growing and would shift more to the jurisdiction in future. The Steering Committee met regularly until 1988 when it was reorganized as the Board of Directors, consistent and on a par with other jurisdictional agencies in the Southeast.

Besides Dr. Watson, the other Steering Committee member from South Carolina was the Rev. Needham Williamson. Mike said:

Needham was a valuable member and made several trips to New York with a small group representing the committee. His most historic contribution was selecting a name for our organization. Before we settled on a name, we were known by a number of informal names, e.g., SEJ Work Team Committee, Volunteer Service Committee, and others. The committee considered the issue of a name for several meetings, but Needham always held out for "Volunteers In Mission" and finally won everyone over to his side. Needham himself recalls that the Presbyterian Church had used the term Volunteers In Mission or VIM. In our committee, members said "Since we have UMCOR, why not also have UMVIM." The idea caught on and UMVIM became the official name of this burgeoning mission effort.

Much later, as other jurisdictions became more active and opened part-time offices in their regions of the country, the name most often used was Volunteers In Mission. In time, the full name of United Methodist Volunteers In Mission became widely used.

At times I felt overwhelmed by a number of nagging questions about the validity and appropriateness of this type of volunteer mission service. It was only as I began to see how God had been at work in the lives of people and saw the enthusiastic response of the hosts, whether here or abroad, that I could affirm the movement and join in with my own enthusiasm. I am glad the UMVIM leaders did not give up on me during those early struggles!

Margaret and I had undertaken this assignment together, realizing that we had very little previous experience with this kind of service. While in Rhodesia we had been hosts to a few volunteers who lived in our home and worked with us on special projects for several months at a time. They were people who came as individuals on their own and were not related officially to any mission program. We did feel, however, that our years of service in Zimbabwe had given us preparation that was basic to the kind of work we would be doing. This seemed to be understood by UMVIM leaders, as they expected we could pick up the dynamics and working philosophy of the movement.

But my struggle to understand the driving force behind this momentum was causing me much anguish, even as I greatly respected the enthusiasm and commitment of the volunteers. It was truly like a conversion when my eyes were opened to see what God was doing in this ministry. Part of my change of heart came about through much reading and reflection on the theology and practice of Christian mission. One of the leading scholars of our time, Bishop Lesslie Newbigin of the Church of England, wrote a statement that leaped out at me. He said, "Every church in every land has a right and responsibility to be in mission to churches in other lands." I think he was saying that even with our affluence and dogmatic manner, we are all still children of God who have a distinct need to be involved in the mission of Christ beyond our national boundaries. That helped me tremendously.

One of the ways I sought to learn more about volunteer ministry was to go first as a regular member of several teams and eventually to lead a number of teams myself. This also brought me face-to-face with several hosts in various communities abroad and at home. It was abundantly clear that the volunteers were welcomed and genuinely invited to join in ministry with locals everywhere they went. I came quickly to appreciate the heavy load of responsibility resting upon team leaders, who serve without any financial remuneration as, of course, do all team members, even giving up their annual vacation time. Indeed, they not only serve without payment, but are responsible for covering their own expenses and contributing to the cost of the project, such as building or medical supplies.

Financial stress on the office was continuing to increase. We were fortunate in those years to have received substantial grants from the SEJ Administrative Council and its predecessor body. Without their generous support, we could not have continued to serve. In some years, almost half our income was from such grants. But I can truthfully say we never questioned that God, who had called us and the many thousands of volunteers who were responding, would provide for our needs in some manner. I believe it is one of the miracles of our day that this has happened when many times it looked so hopeless.

Dr. Watson recalled an early conversation with me.

When you came on board, you asked me what I would advise you to do. I told you that, first, you should learn as much about volunteer activity throughout the jurisdiction as you could, and second, try to help each conference develop a strong conference UMVIM committee. We did not intend to force a particular structure on anyone but help them to become organized.

At that time most of the volunteer activity was not related to our committee, and many people who were heavily involved questioned the need for the office and the organization. Their efforts had been successful, and they did not need the help. One of our first goals was to facilitate their work and make it more effective. Another objective was to introduce the idea of volunteerism to those who had not considered or even heard of this avenue of service.

Spreading the word about the UMVIM movement was always a major concern. As in any new development, it took time for word to get around to people that an office was open for anyone in need of assistance. I was often distressed at how little was known about the UMVIM channel of service, even by the organized church. For example, several years after we came to UMVIM, an interesting letter came to the office from Trinity United Methodist Church in Gainesville, Georgia. Clarence Miller, Trinity's mission chair, had written, "The Reverend Reginald Wheatley, Florida Conference mission secretary, has just sent to me the fall and winter issue of *UMVIM Update*. In a sense, we feel like exclaiming, 'Where have you been all of our life?' since this is the first time to my knowledge that we have received materials like this in the three years I have been mission chairperson." Similar letters came to us from all across the country. The situation began to improve as word spread through the personal experience of volunteers, the jurisdictional UMVIM publications, and in recent years, publicity given through the GBGM and other sources.

As we were getting more involved with UMVIM work, our daughter Carolyn asked me to explain exactly what her mom and I would be doing. I replied jokingly, but with real intent, that we would be putting people to work without remuneration. She replied, "Daddy, you should be good at that because you have been doing it with us kids for a long time!"

CHAPTER FOUR

The World Is Our Parish

Lead on, O King eternal; we follow, not with fears,
For gladness breaks like morning where'er thy face appears.
Thy cross is lifted o'er us; we journey in its light;
the crown awaits the conquest; Lead on, O God of might.

Ernest W. Shurtleff, 1887

Increasing growth was taking place with the movement in the Southeast and the whole country. The Southeastern Jurisdiction UMVIM office was used as a de facto office for Global Ministries as there was no other of its kind in the denomination. The board was also a generous supporter as they simultaneously referred potential volunteers to our office for placement. An increasing number of people wanted to be involved with UMVIM. They wanted to feel that they were working through the connectional structure of the church rather than on their own. This growth in numbers meant we must target areas of need that could be assisted by volunteer activity. At this point we realized that part of our system was not working. In 1977, still our first year as an organization, we had an important consultation with Global Ministries staff in which they promised to provide an "abundance of mission opportunities." This offer was made to us on several occasions, but it just did not happen.

Dr. Watson recalled:

In the original job description for our coordinator, we had specified that he need not make visits to churches outside this jurisdiction, including the overseas areas. Assurances were given that plenty of mission opportunities would be provided by GBGM staff for us to promote. It now seemed, however, that if we were going to be faithful to our stated plan and react only to genuine needs as expressed by overseas church colleagues, the coordinator would need to visit these leaders and interpret the volunteer program to them. The visits would not be to solicit projects open to volunteers, but simply to make churches aware of our existence and what we might provide, and that we were available. We rewrote the job description to include this additional responsibility and mailed it to the Interdivisional Task Force. Hearing no dissent, Tom was authorized by our board to travel overseas and to U.S. mission agencies in order to consult with the leaders.

The Reverend Robert Edmonds, a mission leader in the Holston Conference of East Tennessee, explained the purpose of my overseas visitations this way: "Tom travels here and there trying to create an atmosphere or climate for this movement in which international church leaders would be comfortable." I felt that was an accurate and helpful statement.

During this period and into the future, we faced a pressing need to know what projects would be open to volunteers both here and abroad. This need became one of our major concerns as requests poured in from across the country for such information. We encouraged overseas leaders to make application for volunteers to the appropriate General Board of Global Ministries area secretary who would then forward the applications to us. All too often these requests failed to get through the system in New York, causing considerable frustration in the office as well as for overseas leaders who had requested volunteers. Finally, we asked area secretaries to send us copies of any applications they received. The process worked better for a time. Eventually overseas leaders began sending their original list of openings to us, sometimes with a copy to the board. Later these applications were sent or called in directly to us by overseas churches on a regular basis. Often, however, I contacted Barbara Pessoa of the GBGM staff asking that an Advance special number be assigned to any project for which teams were requested. She was always helpful in doing so.

By October 1977 my frustration in trying to coordinate this movement was at a high level. I was constantly torn between my loyalty to Global Ministries and the responsibility to serve this new grassroots movement. I had grown accustomed in Africa to a rapidly advancing national church leadership with a decreasing emphasis on the use of mission personnel. With UMVIM, it seemed that the reverse was happening.

This frustration led me to draft a statement I referred to as "Obstacles to Coordination," which I sent to our Executive Committee and to Dr. Tracey Jones, chief executive of Global Ministries. This statement included the following six concerns: First, many church leaders and laypeople made their own arrangements with overseas leaders without informing the UMVIM office or the board office in New York. Second, Global Ministries had failed to supply us with current lists of volunteer mission opportunities as promised. Third, Global Ministries had made personnel available for the SEJ regional office, yet its World Division was not itself actively engaged in utilizing volunteers. Fourth, we were not sure where we belonged—to the GBGM, which paid our salary, or to the UMVIM-SEJ Steering Committee that directed our work. Fifth, United Methodist Committee on Relief (UMCOR), a Global Ministries agency, had its own staff handling volunteers for emergencies; however, UMCOR's support of the UMVIM-SEJ was uncertain. Sixth, and last, the UMVIM-SEJ office was frequently called upon by Global Ministries and other jurisdictions to work out placements for volunteers without giving UMVIM any official recognition or financial assistance as a national office for volunteer services.

Many questions also weighed heavily on my mind at that time. First, how could middle-class Americans work alongside nationals in severely depressed areas of the world in a spirit of mutuality? Second, what attitudes and extra baggage did they take with them? Third, what was the average volunteer's understanding of the Christian faith in a global context? Fourth, what preparation and training were volunteers receiving? Fifth, what difference was their brief service making in their lives upon their return? Sixth, what did their hosts think of their ministry? Seventh, and last, how did their ministry enable and empower others to serve?

Tracey Jones, the retired head of the GBGM's World Division, recalled his own reflection about these concerns: "It was Mike Watson's brainchild to send short-term missionaries overseas, but it would not have come to life without the encouragement and support of Harry Haines and the directors of the United Methodist Committee on Relief. The fact that Mike was from South Carolina established from the very first days a unique Southeastern Jurisdiction connection that has held to this day."

Dr. Lois Miller, who followed Jones as head of the GBGM's World Division, remembered:

In the early days, before the movement became known as Volunteers In Mission, when people from local churches were determined to become more involved in mission endeavors, it was local initiative from the beginning rather than a 'top down' program. At the same time, the potential to continue an attitude of 'helping' was thought by mission-board staff to be a deterrent to the changing concept of mutuality in mission. Some regular missionaries voiced this concern too. I believe you and your leaders began to make a difference in developing concepts which led the general church to buy into the opportunities. I recall our joint efforts in orientation, communication, educational sessions, and staff assignment for the movement. We knew voluntarism was to be the wave of the future, and the Christian commitment to be involved with sisters and brothers around the world was the church's response! God bless all of those people who caught the vision and responded with their talents.

Dr. Charles Germany, assistant to Lois Miller, was also of great assistance to us. He has written that UMVIM leaders "blazed new trails in positioning dedicated persons and resources of our church here to mission in the larger world."

As the SEJ office was serving as an unofficial central referral point throughout the country in the early years, we approached Dr. Miller, suggesting that the SEJ office be recognized as the World Division volunteer office. She responded that volunteerism was not a priority for the World Division.

With no central coordinating office, the movement eventually grew into a proliferation of small offices in several jurisdictions with none able to serve as a national voice or presence. UMCOR, a national agency, received most of the publicity in the event of disasters, but relied almost entirely on volunteers to get its work done. The UMVIM movement had no way to put forward its case to the general church public as did UMCOR, although the UMVIM-SEJ office until quite recently supplied much of the personnel in this disaster-relief ministry.

By the spring of 1979, Margaret and I had to come to a decision about our future. The General Board of Global Ministries' commitment to three years of salary support would end that June. Their faithful support in this initial period had been invaluable. We had several options. One was to offer for another overseas assignment with the World Division, which appeared to be favorable for us. A second was to return to the pastorate in my home South Georgia Conference, which had much appeal for me. A third option was to accept the invitation from the UMVIM Steering Committee and the SEJ Executive Committee to remain on as coordinators. I was leaning heavily in the direction of the pastorate and had contacted my own Bishop William R. Cannon about my interest. As we struggled with this issue, Margaret asked me if I was going to do what God wanted or what I wanted. We finally agreed to offer ourselves for further service, with the understanding that it would take a number of years to get the movement well established. This was an act of faith for all of us, as there was little ground for sound financial support. But with Bishop Joel McDavid and Bishop G. Earl Hunt Jr., and the SEJ Executive Committee behind us, along with Dr. Watson and the UMVIM Committee, we together made that commitment to the future, believing that this movement is indeed the work of God.

This decision, of course, led to the issue of funding for the office. We received our last salary check from Global Ministries in June 1979. The board had extended our salary support one year longer than originally promised. We resigned from the World Division at that time and were then in a position to give full-time service as UMVIM coordinators for the Southeast.

The Steering Committee established our salaries and related expenses in the budget which, looking back now, was quite small. But it was still a major struggle to raise the necessary funds. UMVIM gained acceptance as an Advance Special with the GBGM's World Division, National Division, and UMCOR. This helped the churches that preferred giving through Advance Specials. We worked continually to raise the budget. Many churches that gave generously to our support over the years of missionary service in Rhodesia continued to support our new work with UMVIM.

Meanwhile, Dr. Watson was taking time to handle the increasing calls for information about medical service. We agreed that this phase of work would be handled by the office in Atlanta in frequent consultation with him. The newsletter *The Knock* would now become the official voice of the Medical Fellowship; it is currently the only medical bulletin of its kind known to us, in our denomination.

In 1980 an invitation came to Dr. Watson from the Jamaica District of the Methodist Church to come there for a visit and discussion regarding possible medical volunteer services where many construction, teaching, and evangelism teams had been working. He reported, "I found a well-organized committee had been at work, and proposed a pattern of helping seven churches in the Kingston area to strengthen their outreach."

Dr. George Evans of Dublin, Georgia, has also been a major partner with us in the medical arena. He has been coordinating volunteer medical teams to St. Ann's Bay Hospital for many years. A wing at this government facility has been named for him. Many more opportunities for medical personnel in other countries began to open quickly.

By 1980 Margaret and I had devoted four years to this fascinating and far-reaching ministry. We were constantly amazed at the way in which God seemed to be at work along every step of our journey. There were no signposts to follow. We were blazing a new trail. I will always be indebted to my friend Mike Watson for his constant encouragement and willingness to stand beside us. Along with many others, we struggled to be responsible to all concerned, yet to keep alive the spontaneous spirit synonymous with Volunteers In Mission. UMVIM-SEJ board members, conference committees, SEJ officials and mission secretaries, and other church leaders were also very supportive, financially as well as with their ideas and suggestions. But it is God who was in charge and to whom all praise is due. The world had, indeed, become our parish!

CHAPTER FIVE

Struggle for Growth and Stability

Through waves and clouds and storms,
God gently clears the way;
wait thou God's time;
so shall this night soon end in joyous day.

Paul Gerhardt, 1653;
trans. by John Wesley, 1739 (Ps. 37:5)

As has been noted, in UMVIM's early years there was little sympathy for the volunteer movement among some of the GBGM staff, who pointed out their perspectives on perceived problems and weaknesses in the movement, such as racism, sexism, and lack of preparation of many volunteer groups. Of course these were real problems. They needed attention. My response, however, was, "Come along and help us with this so we can accomplish the work of God in a manner that is appropriate." The appeal seemed to fall on deaf ears.

With the approach of the 1980 General Conference, John Trundle and others suggested that we in the UMVIM-SEJ propose legislation to that body. The petition would call for two actions:

1. To affirm Volunteers In Mission as a valid form of mission
2. To instruct the General Board of Global Ministries to become actively involved and supportive of this work.

I was in the Mission Committee at General Conference when the proposal was passed. It was never discussed on the floor of General Conference at all, but passed immediately without debate, bringing many of us considerable relief. (The vote in committee was ninety-nine for passage and only one abstention.)

Dr. Mike Watson, a General Conference delegate from South

Carolina, had been waiting eagerly for the committee's report to come before the whole body. He likes to recall that "when the proposal came to the floor and was passed without comment and without a dissenting vote, I relaxed—and one of the finest speeches ever planned for presentation at General Conference died unspoken. At long last, we were a part of the church!"

A few weeks later Betsy Ewing, chief executive of Global Ministries, called me to New York for a special committee meeting at which the chief executives of the various divisions would respond and react to the action of the General Conference. Several of the participants knew little of the volunteer movement, while others were uncertain about how to carry out their mandate. When my turn came to respond to the group, I concentrated on saying what a golden opportunity the board would be missing if it failed to recognize this new day in mission in the life of our church. I stressed that many people do want to participate personally and are not satisfied by just sending their money to mission agencies. They want to be involved, with hands-on experience.

The year 1980 was also significant as the year of our first UMVIM rally at Lake Junaluska, which has continued every year since and has become the annual highlight of the movement in the Southeast, eagerly anticipated by many participants. At the conclusion of each rally, Mike Watson would say to me, "Tom, I believe this was the best one yet!" Volunteers come from across the South and elsewhere to tell their own personal mission stories. Prominent national and international leaders have been invited to share their faith and inspiration, such as Bishops Raul Ruiz and Ulises Hernandez of Mexico, Paulo Mattos of Brazil, Christopher Jokomo of Zimbabwe, Mvume Dandala of South Africa, and others such as the presidents of the MCCA, the Reverends Claude Cadogan, Edwin Taylor, Eric Clarke, William Watty, and Bruce Swapp. In my opinion, the rally is one of the most powerful spiritual experiences in our church today.

By October of that year, following General Conference endorsement, an official report was presented at the GBGM annual meeting which recognized that action "was introduced by groups wishing to energize and facilitate the development of the movement of volunteers within United Methodism." This, in turn, made it "mandatory that the board policy and program regarding short-term volunteers be coordinated and accelerated. Some serious challenges and shifts in volunteer programs [had] occurred in recent years."

Three and one-half years later, after General Conference action, Global Ministries established its own VIM office with a part-time secretary and two field representatives. Unfortunately, hardly anyone on the planning committee for the new office and staff had any significant experience with volunteers in mission. Thus, that arrangement only lasted a few years and was discontinued. UMVIM, being a grassroots movement, had its own sponsorship in the jurisdictions and conferences, which were not involved in plans for a board office. Hence, the movement was resistant to the prospect of outside control which this plan seemed to envision.

The following year, the second rally was held at Lake Junaluska and once again the enthusiastic response of participants confirmed that we were on the right track in providing such a forum for volunteers to gather and share their enthusiasm for mission. The attendance was more than three hundred. Back in 1978 and 1979, UMVIM had been given one evening during the annual SEJ Conference on Christian Mission to present the program, but it was quickly realized that a full weekend was necessary to provide the training and information needed.

At all of these early rallies, we invited chief leaders of Global Ministries, US mission agency staff and overseas colleagues to share their understanding of this developing mutual ministry. A number of countries in particular were invited to send representatives, such as the Reverend Edwin Taylor, president of the Methodist Church in the Caribbean and the Americas. In his address, he raised the issue of motivation, saying, "I hope you, with all of your zeal that you have when you go to work in these areas, ask yourselves searching questions such as, 'What am I really doing? Is this a total expression of my concern for the areas where I am going?' If we really wish to help these churches, we must seek to help the communities and the islands where they are, in a holistic manner that recognizes the many barriers to our progress often caused by friendly nations." Taylor was quick to remind his listeners of the enormous but sacrificial aid given to our church in the US in the transfer of many of their much-needed clergy to our shores. "I ask you who come in the name of Jesus Christ with the love of God in your hearts to open your eyes and understand the causes of our incessant poverty."

Taylor went on to say, "Your work, your prayers, your gifts, and your people are needed and appreciated. However, always keep in mind the real, difficult, and underlying structural problems we face in the Caribbean. So we need to look at this open sore with open eyes, love and, understanding."

During this period of struggle and growth, we constantly learned from our partners in mission at home and abroad. A church leader who spoke at the 1983 rally was the Reverend Reginald Ponder, SEJ executive secretary. He said, "When we go to serve, we bear an enormous burden of representing not only ourselves and Christ, but the whole of our church. Others, seeing us, see our church. Ponder recalled being on a mission to Jamaica when work was proceeding normally on expanding a church building near Spanish Town. He, like all the team, had dirt covering his clothes and body, and sweat was running down his face. A well-dressed young Jamaican man came by several times, finally expressing with amazement, 'I have never seen a white man working like you are doing.' This made a profound impression on me."

By 1997 the annual rally had become the jurisdiction's principal mission conference. An incredible bond of friendship and trust has built up among volunteers, reinforced by the annual rallies for the jurisdictions and the annual conferences. Church leaders in far-flung places who have invited volunteers into their midst have often said that relationships in UMVIM have helped to strengthen their own sense of identity. For all this, we give God praise.

CHAPTER SIX

Rallying the Cause

God of love and God of power, grant us in this burning hour
grace to ask these gifts of thee, daring hearts and spirits free.
God of love and God of power, thou hast called us for this hour.

Gerald H. Kennedy, ca. 1939

One of our most important jobs as coordinators was to gather and maintain an accurate, up-to-date list of available opportunities for voluntary mission service for teams and individuals in this country and abroad. We listed these projects in the quarterly newsletter, *UMVIM Update,* which was begun in 1976, our first year in this ministry.

The quarterly listing led to the preparation of a booklet listing projects by jurisdiction for National Division projects; by other countries for the World Division; designated as ecumenical projects or as UMCOR projects, both national and international.

As may be expected, most UMVIM projects relate to some type of construction, for new church buildings or repairs to a parsonage, social hall, school, or clinic. It could be repair to homes of families in difficult situations. It could be related to community projects or disaster relief in the wake of hurricanes, floods, tornadoes, earthquakes, or burned churches. We have tried diligently to keep the listings up-to-date in order to provide current information as needed. Lists are revised at least every two years in printed form. The current *Project List* is available in the UMVIM office in Atlanta for persons planning mission projects.

If anyone wants to participate in a mission project in this denomination, there should be plenty of places where they could serve. Usually it does not take much effort to locate such a place. It was distressing to learn of individuals who were having difficulty finding available service openings that matched with their particular talents. In order to obtain information about potential opportunities for volunteers, I began making visits to nearby countries that seemed likely to be receptive to our ministry.

One of my first overseas visits was in 1977. I was attending the Annual Conference of the Methodist Church in the Caribbean and the Americas along with the Reverend Joseph Perez, an area secretary of the World Division. We got to know each other better and realized how complementary our work could be. One stop on my visit was on the island of Jamaica where the Reverend Evans Bailey, the genial and gracious superintendent, was my host. Barbara Bailey, Evans's wife, and one of their sons went with me over to St. Ann's Bay where the church had long had a desperate need for a new manse.

At St. Ann's we were greeted by the Reverend Stephen and Myrtle Poxon, Welsh missionaries serving under the British Methodist Conference. They made us feel quite at home with a wonderful meal that evening. When Myrtle was showing me to my bedroom, she said, "Tom, you feel free to move your bed around any way you like. It will no doubt be raining tonight; it rained earlier in the day. There are a lot of leaks in this room. So you feel free to move your bed around and try to find a place where it is not leaking!" I think she was trying to tell me of the urgent need for a new roof!

This old manse had been given to the Methodist church many years ago. It was built as a residence for an Anglican priest and was considered to be more than two hundred years old. The story goes that the priest's wife and two daughters were on a boat leaving the harbor to return to England for a visit when their boat capsized and sank. They were lost at sea. The broken-hearted priest returned to England and the church property was turned over to the Methodist Church. They have thirty-eight acres in a wonderful location high in the hills above St. Ann's Bay. But the old house was desperately in need of repairs if it was to be of any further use. When I realized the situation, I thought to myself that I should be able to find an annual conference that would take on the task of joining with the church members in building a new residence. I came back home and gave a call to the chair of the South Georgia Conference UMVIM Committee. They were just in the process of gearing up for their work. David Guest, their chairman, liked the plan and warmly agreed to accept the building project, as did the entire committee. In fact, they promised to send as many as six teams to do the work, each team contributing about $5,000.

I was privileged to be at St. Ann's Bay when one of those teams was working there. What a wonderful fellowship was developing between the locals and the visitors. There was no sense of "us" and "them," but a sharing of friends working together on the project for their church.

The MCCA met again in Kingston a few years later after the building was finished. As was customary for the conference program, they planned to have a day apart on Saturday. So that day everybody went over to St. Ann's Bay to attend the opening and dedication of the manse. It was dedicated free of debt.

At the dedication of the new residence, Superintendent Evans Bailey was eager not only to thank those of us who were there representing UMVIM but also to affirm his own people, recognizing that they had put more into the project in terms of hard labor, gifts-in-kind, and cash than had anyone from outside. He expressed his deep thanks for the sacrifices they had made and for the friendships that had developed with team members, for the strengthening of Christian ties across the seas and across racial barriers. It was tremendously uplifting to hear him affirm the local church members and not just recognize the contribution of those who came from other shores.

Bailey has been one of the strongest supporters of this movement. He said, "We are in a new missionary era, not in the mission field of the nineteenth century. Gone is the old paternalistic approach of big, powerful, affluent persons from the USA who come and tell the people what to do. The volunteers who come and work will also benefit," pointed out Bailey. "The deep spiritual vitality and Christian commitment [of the Jamaican people] challenges them. We have learned there is an integrity in receiving as well as an integrity in giving, which makes sense of the whole matter of Christian witness and mission." Referring to construction projects, he said, "In every case, the building is the visible aspect of the program. The invisible, yet very potent aspect of the program, has to do with sharing the Christian experience."

The St. Ann's project had been referred to us through UMCOR, which was at that time using volunteers more than any other agency in our denomination. Harry Haines, UMCOR's former executive, made a special effort to increase the use of volunteers in projects like this. Joe Perez was present at the dedication as a representative from the World Division. He asked me, "Tom, why was this an UMCOR project and not a World Division project?" and I said, "You could probably answer that question better than I," for I, too, wondered why it seemed so difficult for such projects to be processed to us by the World Division. UMCOR was organized to deal with emergency situations, not routine building projects like a new parsonage. But this project came to us through UMCOR, showing me that if we were going to get anything done, we would have to get the projects through UMCOR or find them ourselves.

On another occasion the UMCOR office in New York called to talk with me about an urgent project in the Dominican Republic that they felt needed attention. It was the rebuilding of an orphanage that had been destroyed by a recent hurricane. My caller said, "Tom, please don't get people excited in the Dominican Republic about the possibility of someone coming. Let's be sure they are going to do it first." I had no intention of stirring up unfounded promises. I went to the Florida Conference thinking they might be the best ones to tackle this need because they had Spanish-speaking people available and were themselves near that island. The Florida Conference agreed to undertake the project. And it was a joy to see that happen.

I had a chance to visit the Dominican Republic while one of the teams was at work on the orphanage renovations. Some of the folk told me how sick some of the volunteers were with dysentery. It was difficult for them to get up and carry on in their work. I heard volunteers themselves say that when they were having a struggle to get up out of bed in the morning because they felt so weak, some of the little children would come around and grab them by the hand and say, "Come on now and get up. You have to help us get our house back together." And with that kind of word the guys would tumble out of bed and get back on the job, sick or not!

Eventually the project was completed and many thanks were given to God and all the people who helped, both locals and visitors. That particular project was under the auspices of the Social Committee of the Christian Council of the Dominican Republic. Soon afterwards at the 1984 General Conference in Baltimore, the superintendent of the Evangelical Church of the Dominican Republic looked me up. He identified himself as the Reverend Hernan Gonzalez Roca and said how grateful he was for the help we had given on the orphanage. Then he asked if we would be interested in giving help to some of their church projects. And I said, "Tell me about your church." The church, he said, was made up of a union of Methodists, Moravians, and Presbyterians; and they received an annual grant from the General Board of Global Ministries. Soon we began sending a constant flow of teams to the Evangelical Church, which has brought much blessing to all involved.

As UMVIM's work was growing, we were always pressed to look for new sources of income. In 1989, retired Bishop R. Kern Eutsler agreed to join the UMVIM staff as our first part-time director of interpretation and promotion. Early in his work, Bishop Eutsler served with a team to Jamaica to experience the volunteer in mission personally in order to interpret this movement with more authenticity. Bishop Eutsler was an effective and committed ally who sought to build a solid base of financial support. He established the Fellowship of One Thousand to which individuals and churches could belong if they had given a minimum of $100 annually for support of the UMVIM ministry. He also designed an attractive lapel pen and certificate to be given to all contributors. Bishop Eutsler served seven years before retiring a second time.

Looking back over that time, Bishop Eutsler said, "My years with UMVIM were among the happiest of my professional life. It is a movement in which I enthusiastically believe. I am convinced it does more to promote the world mission of the church than any other program we have. In addition to what volunteers mean to our mission centers around the world, even if there were no other benefits, the life-changing effect UMVIM has on the volunteers would be enough to make it worthwhile."

CHAPTER SEVEN

Sisters and Brothers Together

Building Relationships

Blest be the tie that binds Our hearts in Christian love;
The fellowship of kindred minds Is like to that above.

John Fawcett, 1782

The building of personal relationships with mission leaders in this country and elsewhere in the world has been vital in the strong and continuous growth of the UMVIM movement since its beginning.

After prayerful and careful study of the overall situation, I began work as facilitator and interpreter for this emerging grassroots ministry by seeking out bishops and other church leaders in Caribbean and Central American countries, traveling to visit with them to explain the ministry and to seek their understanding and cooperation. At times I went with potential volunteer team leaders representing several annual conferences in the USA. We would sit down with interested church officials for a few days of visiting and sharing and developing ties of friendship. Over the years the ministry has spread beyond nearby lands to many countries around the world. All of our host churches have been very affirming of the work of the volunteers, extending gracious invitations to come and share in their ministry.

At first I hesitated seeking out relationships with overseas church leaders, as I understood it was the responsibility of Global Ministries to develop those contacts and openings for volunteers. The seeking out of such relationships was not easy in the beginning as this was frowned upon by Global Ministries staff. Only when the UMVIM-SEJ office realized that it would be necessary for me to make such visits were they begun. As a result, strong ties with potential host churches have become the foundation of the movement's growth and vitality.

A consultation in 1977 in Atlanta with representatives from the Global Ministries was called to deal with the issue of openings for volunteers, which proved fruitless. At a 1982 conference of the Methodist Church in the Caribbean of the Americas at which I was present, a discussion was held at great length regarding a possible consultation between that church and The United Methodist Church on the subject of volunteer service. MCCA leaders insisted that representatives from several church agencies such as UMVIM and the General Board of Discipleship participate as well as the General Board of Global Ministries. Bishop F. Herbert Skeete suggested that all of these groups including UMVIM be invited to meet in Puerto Rico, where he was the episcopal leader, in order to promote full dialogue with all the main partners involved in volunteer ministries.

The meeting was held in Puerto Rico but again not much progress was made. The Global Ministries staff continued to maintain that they would provide us with details and up-to-date information regarding the opportunities for volunteers to serve in different parts of the world. Very little information was forthcoming.

Nothing of any significance developed out of the proposed consultation. Shortly thereafter, I went to New York to meet with Dr. Tracey Jones, who then was the general secretary of the Board of Missions, asking for help in this matter. He suggested that I go to see World Division area secretaries, directly seek their cooperation, and obtain that information. I told him I would certainly do so, but I was not hopeful of gaining much of a sympathetic hearing. I did solicit that kind of cooperation from each of the area secretaries on a visit to New York as well as in correspondence. Unfortunately, very little ever came from the New York staff to us. In fact, I can remember only three projects, all in Mexico, that came through the World Division for UMVIM teams, and a few others that came in later through the Volunteers In Mission office established by Global Ministries. The vast majority of projects were sought out and identified by our own office.

In the beginning of our work as coordinators, Margaret and I felt that working through the World Division was the best way to proceed. It soon proved to be unworkable. The main problem was one of timing. Prospective volunteers, especially professional people, urgently needed an immediate response to their inquiries about future service to fit in with their busy schedules. Action had to be taken by the most direct and fastest route. This did not allow time for going through another loop to make arrangements for a prompt placement. The same time constraints applied to the matter of funding. There is a vast difference between handling the work of career missionaries and that of short-term volunteers. The GBGM staff were working with salaried personnel on long-term assignment. The UMVIM office was responding to urgent calls for a placement within a few weeks or months, but for short periods of time. UMVIM requests demanded a prompt response if many professionally trained, committed volunteers would be able to serve at all.

I took the matter up with our UMVIM Executive Committee, which felt the time had come for me to begin making regular overseas trips. I had made a couple of visits, but only in cooperation with and at the expense of the Board of Global Ministries. The committee now felt it was necessary for me to undertake these trips using UMVIM funds. I had to plan very carefully where and when to go to discuss plans with overseas leaders who were becoming increasingly involved with us in this ministry.

In March of 1983 a consultation between the MCCA and Global Ministries did take place in New York. The focus was to be on Volunteers In Mission. Since Margaret and I were the only persons working in our denomination who had this program as their sole responsibility, I fully expected to be present and participate. The invitation, however, was not extended. Had I been invited, perhaps my experience in matching volunteers to service opportunities in overseas areas could have been helpful. But it was clear that the Global Ministries staff intended that the volunteer movement be channeled through its New York offices.

Reports from the March 1983 consultation indicated a negative tone to the work of UMVIM. Apparently no one from this country who had first-hand knowledge of the volunteer movement was present to interpret how the ministry seeks to work. Eventually, however, our overseas colleagues would turn directly to the UMVIM-SEJ office in Atlanta with their invitations to share in ministry.

I went to General Conferences, Global Gatherings, and other large meetings and talked with leaders from other parts of the world. These were always wonderful occasions when we sat down together, became acquainted, and began to understand and appreciate each other and the ministries we represented.

Another meeting that seemed to hold potential for UMVIM interpretation was the quadrennial United Methodist Men's Congress at Purdue. I have attended each of these congresses regularly since we returned home in 1976 and have always found men there from other parts of the world and from the United States who were eager to know about the UMVIM ministry. I took a display to my first congress at Purdue in 1977 and gave out information about the movement to all who were interested. The men asked me to lead workshops at Purdue to explain this new avenue of mission. The UMVIM movement seems to have great appeal to men in general and I wanted to be in attendance at the men's major events lifting up this challenging lay movement.

The United Methodist Men of North Georgia Conference may have been the most active in this ministry of any conference in the country. Their work has been both national and international. At home they have concentrated on constructing church facilities, setting up plans for disaster response in flood and hurricane relief, helping restore burned churches, and serving in more personal ways such as evangelism and teaching. Abroad, North Georgia's men have served primarily in Mexico, Central and South America, Africa, Europe, and the Caribbean. For several years now, the North Georgia Conference has had its own full-time mission secretary.

On one occasion I was asked by the president of United Methodist Men of the Southeast if I would organize an overseas trip for their conference presidents and the national secretary, James Sneed, to a nearby area. We consulted with the president of the MCCA, the Reverend Edwin Taylor, who suggested we visit Jamaica. Most conference presidents and their wives were able to participate. We arrived in Kingston to an enthusiastic welcome by our host, the Reverend Terrence Rose. This opened the door for much future work to be done by men's groups from all across the United States. It also helped to internationalize the men's entire program.

"I have received far more than I was able to give," volunteers say when they return home. And, "I will never be the same again." The learning that comes from this shared fellowship is that "mission is a two-way street." This expression is most often used, especially by new volunteers, as their eyes are opened to the fact of Christ's presence long before they arrived on the scene, and for the vital witness of people they find in many other places beyond their own homes. These words are spoken as if an electric light has been suddenly turned on in their minds!

Wonderful bonds of fellowship and love have been developed with colleagues around the world. One of the great blessings is to be able to pick up the phone and talk to many of these church leaders as personal friends and converse about the work that needs to be done. I wish there were space to mention many church leaders from other countries who have been keen to work with us, but this has been true in every country in which we have served. If problems arise, they usually can be resolved quickly. If an individual is eager to serve, it is often possible to handle the red tape quickly and make a placement in a short time. The telephone and fax machine are used frequently in trying to work out a prompt placement for teams and individuals.

It is difficult to overestimate the importance of up-to-date communication with our colleagues here or abroad who serve as our hosts. In considering any place where volunteers may go to serve, it is essential to have the correct information about the project: Is this project a viable one? Has it the backing of the local officials? Are the necessary building materials or medical supplies available? Are adequate housing and food arrangements on site? From hard experience, we learned the necessity of careful advance planning.

On occasion, failure to plan has resulted in disaster. Serious problems, for example, resulted when building teams were sent out through Global Ministries for a large national building project in Panama months before preparations had been made, despite warnings that the construction site was not ready. Some teams insisted that they go, even though they were told that the ground was not ready for excavation work. These teams had terrible frustration, and in the end had to be assigned to other projects or accept heavy airline fees for changing their return airline tickets.

Just as we recognize the importance of building personal relationships with host churches, it is important to build close ties between traditional and volunteer missioners. Each needs and deserves the support and cooperation of the other. Bonds of solidarity need to be strengthened in the handling of these two forms of mission service.

The year 1988 brought a major change in UMVIM leadership in the Southeast. Dr. Mike Watson retired after twelve devoted years of securing this young movement upon a solid foundation. He was then elected to serve as medical coordinator for the SEJ, and continued on the Board of Directors as president emeritus. His successor was Dr. John T. Martin, Jr., a distinguished pastor in the Virginia Conference who, for the next eight years, provided exciting and creative leadership. This year also marked our becoming one of the seven official agencies of the SEJ Administrative Council with our own Board of Directors.

As a pastor in the Virginia Conference, Jack Martin and his wife, Marianne, participated in their first UMVIM trip with a team led by Doug and Doris True, who had pioneered volunteer mission work in Northern Virginia. The Martins were excited to be traveling to Haiti. Jack later reported:

> Our UMVIM experience in Haiti left us unable to go on with life in the same glib way we had previously been living. I was exhausted, spiritually troubled, and unresolved in my mind as to what anyone could do to make a difference when the odds were so heavily against any real change. Little did I know at that time what a marvelous thing was stirring in God's kingdom. Volunteers In Mission was in its fledgling stages. There were few visionaries and a lot of concern about what it might mean if untrained laypeople and naive, albeit well-intentioned, clergy started going out into the mission field. Voices of warning were being sounded, but there was a spirit moving that could not be stopped. The best that could be hoped for would be that they could somehow be harnessed.

Dr. Martin's description of the UMVIM movement spoke worlds about the growth taking place in this ministry across the country. I am reminded of the saying, "The church exists by mission like fire exists by burning." We are participants here in a grassroots movement that is powerful and all-consuming. Dr. Martin went on to say:

The establishment of the UMVIM-SEJ office within the structure of the United Methodist Church is well documented in other parts of this book, but suffice it to say that this was one of the wisest decisions made in the mission movement in this century. God was raising up a grassroots movement to meet the needs of hurting people not only in Haiti but in countless other places in the world, including the United States. By God's grace, I was named chairperson of the Virginia Conference UMVIM Committee and soon met our SEJ Coordinator. Our work expanded quickly into a number of new areas.

As Dr. Martin's participation in the movement grew, so did his understanding of many of the issues involved. He said:

We have learned that our work is but a vehicle to put us in touch with God's people, to bring about better understanding, to sow hope, and to build bridges of peace. While the work of our hands is important, in some ways it is secondary to a greater purpose of bringing people together to witness what God can do. The UMVIM movement is unique in that it is a people-to-people program. Not only do teams work together with their host church, but they worship, pray, live, laugh, and cry together. I often caution potential team members that they risk having their lives changed forever if they go on a mission team.

We discovered that sometimes we could manage some big projects by sending multiple teams, one after another. This approach made it possible to assist in the building of a large church at San Lucas Atoyatenco, Mexico, and a home for the aging in Mexico City. It was during our work in both Haiti and Mexico that we came to realize the importance of working in partnership with our hosts. We soon discovered that we did not have to worry about whether we would find Christ in the places we visited: as a matter of course Christ would already be well at work before our arrival.

I want to share two experiences that bespeak the wonder of what God is doing through UMVIM. The first relates to an invitation the Virginia Conference had from Bishop Peter Storey of South Africa to come to his country to help build a church in one of the "homelands" to which thousands of Africans had been relocated from their ancestral lands. The people welcomed us graciously, but also with a certain shyness. The hostess for Marianne and me was the president of the Methodist women's group, who had us housed in the home of one of her daughters.

The team's work was to help construct a rural church in an area where lived a number of European or Afrikaner families. Before the team had finished its work, some of the local whites became so interested in seeing this team of whites and blacks working together that they joined in to help. Remember, this was in the day when apartheid was fully enforced and little social contact took place between the races.

On our final day at the work site, we gathered inside the new church with excited people for the service of dedication with Bishop Storey presiding. At the close of the very moving service, the Americans were asked to linger in the front while the villagers exited the building. When we finally came out the door, we saw the entire congregation formed into a huge circle, waiting to greet us one by one with hugs, tears, and looks too deep for words. It was late in the day when the last of our group finished moving down the line of greeters. Moments later we got into the vans and drove off into the majestic South African sunset. The following Sunday we were attending worship at the downtown Johannesburg Central Methodist Mission. Pastor Storey in commending our service issued a challenge for that congregation to consider doing the same.

In 1995, at the annual UMVIM-SEJ rally at Lake Junaluska, one of the keynote speakers was the Reverend Mvume Dandala, former pastor of the Central Mission and now elected as Presiding Bishop of the Methodist Church of Southern Africa. He began by talking about a work team from Virginia that had helped build a church in a South African homeland. After he described what had been done, speaking about the sanctity of labor, he said, 'I have an announcement. We now have, in Southern Africa, SAMVIM— Southern Africa Methodist Volunteers In Mission, and we are doing what you do!' Things had come full circle on that day, for sure.

A second experience that I will describe took place in 1993 in Ivanovo,

Russia, where we had gone to do renovation work at a children's tuberculosis sanitorium. As we passed between the buildings, we noticed the faces of children in the windows watching us. We waved and they waved back. When we had gathered for a welcome in a small, crowded room, a beautiful girl of six or seven, clothed in a festive folk dress, stepped forward with a gift of salt and a large loaf of bread to offer us this traditional Russian greeting of hospitality. After we had eaten, the children and their teachers entertained us with songs, dances, and skits. Several boys brought us homemade gifts carved from the bark of trees in the forest. This was the beginning of one of the most wonderful experiences of my life. People I had been brought up to fear were now taking a group of Americans into their hearts.

Young people [in Russia] are searching for where the truth can be found. There was a lot of interest in what we believed. One young woman asked me, 'What is a Methodist?' On the last evening of our visit before heading home via Moscow, a banquet was held during which many speeches were given by team members and our gracious hosts remembering the highlights of our time together. Near the end of the evening, the woman in charge of the language interpreters stood to speak. Her English was flawless. She spoke words of gratitude for the experience her students had had, and not just for the chance to be interpreters, but more for the experience of coming to know us personally. She implied that she was not a Christian, but then said the most remarkable thing: "I believe you were sent by Someone I do not yet know."

I thought to myself, "Lord, God Almighty, as we live and breathe, we were surely meant to be in this place at this time." Since then I have struggled to maintain an annual American Christian presence in that city, to continue this work of love and witness in the hope that others would also sense that "Someone they did not know" was working on their behalf, who wanted to know and love them intimately so that one day they too could proclaim "the Name that is above every name," even Jesus Christ.

Succeeding Dr. Martin as the third president of the UMVIM-SEJ Board of Directors in 1996 was C. Leroy Irwin, a layman from Tallahassee, Florida. Leroy had previously chaired the Florida UMVIM Committee for a number of years, had led many teams and brought Mexican young people to live in his home while pursuing their education. One of his favorite projects is developing district UMVIM committees as a means of keeping close to the grassroots.

Gradually over the years, a spirit of cooperation has grown between the UMVIM movement and the General Board of Global Ministries in the placement of volunteers. Both groups have come to realize that the call of mission places heavy responsibility upon the administrative resources of Global Ministries and UMVIM leaders. Both agencies have operated from much the same general mission philosophy of full respect for our hosts and working only in response to their specific invitations to a mutual ministry. Emphasis on selection and proper training of would-be missioners is also a constant concern.

UMVIM offices across the country continue to be the major channels for placement of volunteers through The United Methodist Church in the USA and abroad. In its outreach across the world, UMVIM has continually stressed the critical importance of personal ties with hosts everywhere. This concept of mutual respect was developed early in the UMVIM ministry of friends working together as sisters and brothers in the name of Christ. The approach has proved to be extremely valuable and is helping to create an attitude of openness and a bond of love and respect across barriers of culture and geography.

CHAPTER EIGHT

Sending Forth

Selection, Placement, Orientation, and Debriefing of Volunteers

Then I heard the voice of the Lord saying,
"Whom shall I send, and who will go for us?"
And I said, "Here am I; send me."

Isaiah 6:8

As a mission movement, UMVIM has evolved naturally over a number of years in a grassroots response to human need. This is just the opposite of a top-down kind of development. The major approach in the beginning and even now is that teams or individuals or couples go to serve for short periods, where invited, in an area of need, usually beyond their own community. The program format has been expanded in response to requests by individuals and couples for more intense involvement for longer periods of time. Interest in volunteer ministry continues to grow. Teams, however, obviously make up by far the largest number of participants.

The Team Concept

One of the first teams from the Wyoming Conference of Northeast Pennsylvania went to Zimbabwe in 1992. It was a large group of twenty-six volunteers with diverse skills and talents including a doctor, a dentist, a librarian, an audiologist, three pastors, three bee keepers, two agriculturalists, five Christian educators, a seamstress, a lab technician, six nurses, and a student. From this initial contact with the Zimbabwe Conference many other forms of mission partnership have developed.

UMVIM projects are usually sponsored by local churches or

annual conferences that underwrite the project and assume responsibility for its outcome. All teams are self-supporting, usually paying their own expenses and contributing toward cost of materials and supplies for the chosen task. This, of course, is in addition to the work and contributions to be made by their hosts.

The team has become a popular format for mission service with groups of ten to twelve or more joining to complete some project, construction or repair of a building. Appropriate personnel must be chosen, with well-qualified leaders and a good balance of skills among team members. That does not mean necessarily that all team members on a construction project must be professional builders, but the team should include an appropriate number of workers with training and experience for the specific task at hand.

A former director of volunteer services of the National Division of Global Ministries has stated his thoughts on this subject:

It is a shared mission, which can have far more Christian impact than going to do a task, completing it, putting in a cornerstone, and departing. The more permanent quality is not bricks and mortar but souls, spirits, insights, and individuals. It is the impact of people coming from afar to be of help because it's the Christ-like thing to do. God is moving within the church, within the nations, and only through openness to his call can we discover his will.

Team selection is always the responsibility of the sponsoring body. If the sponsor is a local church, usually the Committee on Missions or some other committee will be assigned the responsibility of selecting team members and the team leader. The persons chosen generally have had previous experience from their own church or have participated in a volunteer mission project.

Selection of team members is critical. Those responsible for the makeup of the team should bear in mind the Christian character of team members and their commitment to mission through The United Methodist Church. Members will need an understanding and appreciation of other cultures, a willingness to accept certain conditions that are set by their host church, and must be open to new insights of the Christian faith and world church.

Orientation is always an important part of the process. It may take the form of a full-day retreat or several evenings together. Emphasis should be made at this time that culture shock will be experienced upon arrival at the mission site and again upon return home. One helpful resource designed to assist in orientation and training is the *UMVIM Handbook,* which contains important information to help in organizing and planning the work team and carrying out a successful team mission project. The *Handbook* is available from the UMVIM office in Atlanta.

The weakest link in the volunteer ministry may well be inadequate orientation, although most leaders are thorough in preparation of their teams. Careful attention to proper orientation is crucial to a successful outcome. Of course, many people do an excellent job, and many team leaders will be thorough in preparing the team. The same quality of attention to proper orientation is also important for host churches. Both are critical to a productive experience.

Much heavy responsibility rests on the team leader, who will bear the burden of the work and the brunt of any problems that may develop. If the project succeeds, team leaders should get proper recognition; if a major problem should develop, they will probably receive the major blame.

Orientation should take place not only before the team leaves home, but also immediately upon arrival at the project site. This is of utmost importance, even before the first day's work begins. A day or two may be planned for getting acquainted in the community, going to church services, learning to feel at home and adjusting to the new living environment and accommodations. Also during this time team members must have clear instruction about local culture, the history of the community and church, and an appreciation of major differences between cultures. Key local officials should lead the orientation sessions in the field, which may take place more than once while the team is there. The introductory session is necessary almost immediately upon arrival.

One of the worst situations of inadequate orientation that I have heard about was of a construction group from the United States that was working on a building project under hot summer sun. Some members of the team complained about the body odor of local workers and went on strike to keep from having to work side by side with them. The superintendent consulted with the circuit pastor, then went to the team leader and asked the team to leave immediately, which they did. There was no reason for them to stay after this serious violation of basic decency and respect.

A physician told of his dismay at the reaction of some team members toward the evening entertainment that was offered by the local people in a Latin American country. One of the team members expressed his consternation and displeasure at their hosts for taking away time that could be put into the work project. The doctor was disappointed and embarrassed that his colleagues could be so unappreciative of the local folks' efforts to put on their best entertainment for their guests. Such behavior is inexcusable. It clearly points out the vital importance of proper orientation and preparation for volunteer teams, whatever their particular assignment.

During a team's visit to a different culture, many reactions will likely stir one's spirit over and over. Dorothy and Bill Appelgate of Iowa went with a group to Honduras and Guatemala, where they were overwhelmed at so much that was new to them. Dorothy put it this way:

> I experienced many different emotions during the ten to twelve days as we traveled along: joy, sadness, fear, hope, anger, frustration, assurance and peace, all in such a short time. One frustration keeps coming back: As several of us walked the market streets, I saw a mother sitting against a building with her two small children leaning against her. The older little boy, about four or five years of age, was going through her hair, probably picking out head lice; and I was thinking what I could do to help. But I went on by! The next morning as we drove by in the bus, the little family was still in the same place, and I felt sick. They had no place to go and no one to care for them, and we kept on going—and I felt sick inside. God forgive me and have mercy.

Debriefing of volunteers takes place when teams are preparing to return home. Most groups can find a place to stop and have refreshments and fellowship before the final departure. Debriefing may take place on board plane or bus. It is difficult to overestimate the importance of evaluation.

When the UMVIM-SEJ office was established in 1976, it was the first in The United Methodist Church. Records at that stage were almost nonexistent though we were aware of some mission activity by churches working from a local church base. I would estimate approximately fifty teams were serving each year, though only a few reported their work to us. The Southeast now sends more than 2,000 teams annually, with about the same number for the rest of the country. Some conferences (e.g., Virginia and Western North Carolina) have sent more than a hundred teams per year, including many on national disaster-relief efforts.

The inspiring accounts of many groups that have truly sought to relate to their hosts are incredible. Bishop Marshall "Jack" Meadors of Mississippi likes to tell how he first got interested in this movement. "I went with Dr. Mike Watson on a medical mission to Haiti in 1982 to inoculate children at La Gonave, perhaps the most impoverished area of the whole island. I was taught to use an immunization gun. We gave thousands of shots. A year later, Mike told me that the death rate among children in that destitute place had dropped dramatically." Bishop Meadors says that since being assigned as episcopal leader for Mississippi, "UMVIM has been a high priority for me. Here in this state, my goal has been to provide an opportunity for every person I ordain to participate in an UMVIM experience." Meadors himself went with one of the dozen or so conference teams from his area to help on a major project in an impoverished Mexican barrio.

The Individual Volunteer

While the work-team concept is well-known across the church by now, the service and application process for individual volunteers has not been so well-known until recent years, when their numbers started to increase. Persons who serve outside the team structure are usually singles or couples who wish to volunteer for service for two months to two years or longer. It is necessary for them to provide their own financial support, often with the assistance of their home churches. Individuals have served as instructors of English as a second language; home evangelists and Bible teachers; physicians, physician assistants, nurses and other health-care workers; consultants in several fields such as agriculture and computers; teachers and youth workers; and in other specialties. In the past it has often been difficult for interested individuals to know about volunteer service—where and to whom to apply, and what mission opportunities might be available for them. Once I asked a young applicant how she happened to have contacted our UMVIM office. She came from quite a large church and had consulted with several pastors and staff members, but no one knew where to refer her. This amazed me. Then, she said, she finally resorted to looking in the Yellow Pages where we had placed a separate listing for just such a purpose.

Individual volunteers range in age from college students and young adults to retirees. Many are looking for a longer period of service than the normal one or two weeks with a team. For some, the experience will lead to a career change, possibly to a church-related vocation. Others may continue their service as traditional missionaries with the Board of Global Ministries. They are a very exciting and challenging group of people who are eager to learn more about the meaning of their Christian faith and its relevance in today's fast-changing society. Thus UMVIM is providing a groundswell of persons interested in possible long-term mission involvement.

Susan Dupree, daughter of South Georgia pastor Bill Dupree and his wife, Sue, spent a summer in Mexico, which taught her much about God, herself, and the world. She reports, "I worked at Camp Sierra Linda, a Methodist youth camp near Monterrey and was greatly impressed by the Christian lifestyle of the youth there. The change in my environment did not automatically mean that I had changed. I am still the selfish person wherever I go unless I allow the Holy Spirit to set my eyes on others and their needs. God answered my prayers and allowed me to share Christ with others. Then I could relieve missionaries in their work and also gain vision for the world and how God can use me, as well as others."

Ordained clergy members have always been active in this movement as team members and as individuals. A few in retirement have served as pastors in response to specific requests from English-speaking congregations in countries such as Mexico and Brazil. My first experience in working out a placement for an active, ordained United Methodist minister was in 1994 at the request of Bishop Kenneth Carder of the Tennessee Conference. He told me he had a bilingual couple who had been accepted by Global Ministries for service, but for whom funds were not available at that time. Bishop Carder was seeking a suitable placement for the Reverend Phillip Beisswenger and his wife, Sandra, in the UMVIM program. "If you can find a place for them to serve," he said, "I will find the necessary funds for their support." I asked for more details, was told that the pastor himself had worked in Central America and was fluent in Spanish, and that his wife was from Nicaragua and also fluent in English. They appeared competent in every way. I immediately contacted the head of the Methodist Church for the Belize-Honduras District, the Reverend Otto Wade, who was delighted with this offer of service and proceeded with arrangements through their MCCA office in Antigua for the couple to serve the coastal community of La Ceiba, Honduras. Since both were fluent in Spanish and English, their availability was providential as work in that area would require the use of both languages. I informed Global Ministries of the situation, as I did not want this placement to be misinterpreted. Board staff seemed to be appreciative that we were able to work out a placement for the Beisswengers, for a few years at least. Phillip and Sandra's work went exceedingly well through four years of ministry, during which they significantly expanded Methodist ministries on the coast and nearby islands. In their fourth and final year, their monthly stipend came from the Methodist Church of the Belize-Honduras District.

Debra White, a young woman from the Holston Conference, went to Australia. She had a master's degree in social work and was interested in serving in that field. Using her skills in social research, she conducted a survey on child and family abuse in Australia at the request of the Australian Council of Churches. The council appreciated her work and published her findings in book form. Another volunteer, Stacey Delarber from Atlanta, also went to the Australian outback. She worked primarily in the Mount Darwin area and endeared herself to her colleagues for her caring, sensitive ministry.

The application process for individual volunteers involves: (1) completion of a four-page application form, (2) a pastor's letter of recommendation, (3) an interview with someone representing the applicant's annual conference, and (4) a final interview and decision with the UMVIM-SEJ office staff. Once a likely placement has been worked out, the Office of Coordination consults further with the volunteer's pastor, directs in the preparation of a budget, and arranges insurance and other necessary details.

Two orientation sessions are held each year, one in May and the other in November. The May session is designed primarily for those going out in the summer months. The November session is for volunteers who will be leaving for assignment early in the new year.

Every attempt is made to match a person's skill and gifts with a particular location and need. For example, we received a call from Bishop Hans Vaxby of the Northern European Conference about a church structure in Lithuania. The need was for an architect and an engineer to evaluate the old buildings recently released back to their conference from their former Communist leaders. The question was whether to repair the crumbling facilities or tear down and build new ones. We were able to secure the services of both specialties from Illinois. They went and gave a full analysis of the situation to the church authorities in that country, to the great delight of church officials. In this case, our office was responding to a specific request for certain skilled people. But often, it is a case of offering the talents and gifts of a potential volunteer to a prospective church leader at home or abroad.

Linda Chambliss, a special education teacher at St. Simons Island, Georgia, had a strong desire to serve in Latin America and work with children who had learning disabilities. Her parents and her church were eager to support her dream. Linda was assigned to the Ana Gonzada Methodist Children's home in Rio de Janeiro for almost a full year. After her return to the USA, I was in Brazil and visited the home. The children flocked around to ask about Linda and if I knew her. When I told them the story, they gave me hugs and asked me in turn to give Linda a hug. They even showed me the room where they slept and their beds she had showed them how to make. They still had some of the dolls that Linda's friends had sent for them. Linda's ministry was a beautiful example of Christian love in action.

Stories of how people's lives have been changed in the work of Christian mission are surely marvelous. How they have been able to use their peculiar gifts and interests in the work of Christ! Many singles and couples have shared their personal faith in simple ways with the people of Russia, as Peggy and Harry Bennett of Florida did. They wanted to be a part of the Russian community for a while and share their faith as God would open the way, despite the language barrier. They simply sought to be a Christian presence in a land undergoing great social and spiritual upheaval.

Amy Jacobs, a retired English and journalism teacher from Powell, Wyoming, spent nearly three years serving with the Methodist Church on the Caribbean island of Dominica. She reminds us that a picture is worth a thousand words,

> But there aren't enough pictures or words to describe an UMVIM experience. In 1990, I arrived to teach English at the St. Andrew [Methodist] High School near the village of Marigot. Little did I know that I would return for two more eight-month stays, not only to teach English but to serve as librarian at the school and play the organ for church services. My travels with work teams elsewhere and as an individual volunteer have had a profound effect on my own Christian personhood, and I have found a deeper spiritual meaning in life not known before. My life will never be the same.

Almost from its beginning, Africa University (AU) has sparked a keen interest in many potential individual volunteers, and a number have been serving. In its early years, AU officials insisted on using primarily African personnel to make the institution authentically African. So we did not pressure them to accept volunteers until they were ready to do so. The first to serve there through our office (and the first officially recognized at AU) was Dr. Don Hill of Florida A and M University. He had been a missionary in Congo and spoke earnestly with me of his desire to work in this new United Methodist worldwide effort that would serve all of Africa. He seemed well-qualified in every respect, and I was delighted that Dr. John Kurewa, then vice-chancellor of AU, was agreeable to his coming. Don was able to take a large shipment of calculators and other instruments given by a Texas firm for the school. He was quite excited to read the first sentence printed out on a computer by one of his students. It read, "This is the day that the Lord has made. Let us rejoice and be glad in it!"

Due to space limitations, only a few individuals have been mentioned here in an attempt to illustrate the diverse ways in which they serve. The placement of such personnel has become a large part of the work of the UMVIM offices across the country, with the SEJ office carrying most of the load.

As one of the major mission agencies placing volunteers in this country, UMVIM has opened the door of ministry, literally, to thousands of volunteers. What a tremendous satisfaction this has brought to me personally as our church seeks to enlist the whole body of Christ to serve wherever there is the call.

CHAPTER NINE

The Medical Volunteers

God of compassion, source of life and health:
strengthen and relieve your servants,
and give your power of healing
    to those who minister to their *needs.*

From *The United Methodist Hymnal.* "For the Sick."
The Book of Common Prayer, *alt. by Laurence Hull Stookey;*
Alt. © 1989 The United Methodist Publishing House.
Used by permission.

For hundreds of years, Christian physicians and other medical personnel have sought to serve Christ and humanity all across the earth. In our own time, volunteer service in various health professions has become a valuable asset at times of special need. Many medical specialists, physicians, surgeons, nurses, dentists, and others continue to serve year after year as medical volunteers in mission.

Medical teams are usually composed of at least one or two general physicians, a dentist, and several nurses. Small teams can be quite effective because they have basic control of their schedule and need very little special attention. Their services can be invaluable. This work is far more than a bandage response to need, as surgeries are often performed and patient education and ongoing care are provided as much as possible. Some teams have included as many as thirty or more persons assisting regular medical programs already underway at various locations. The basic intent is to supplement any medical service being provided rather than initiating an entirely new project.

Dr. Michael C. Watson, UMVIM medical coordinator for the Southeastern Jurisdiction, is without doubt the leader among physicians seeking to provide volunteer medical service opportunities for all interested persons. He has been involved in medical volunteer missions longer than anyone I know of in The United Methodist Church. Years ago, he was a representative to the National Council of Churches USA and a member of the United Methodist General Board of Global Ministries. As a result of these and other valuable contacts, Dr. Watson has been able to provide critical leadership to this growing movement. He comes with strong church and medical credentials.

A number of medical teams have concentrated on a particular specialty, such as eye care. Dr. Harold Crosswell of Columbia, South Carolina, has been dedicated to this type of ministry. Ophthalmologists, optometrists, and medical support personnel have been involved for more than a dozen years in a remote corner of Haiti, where they have established the most sophisticated eye care on the island. The team usually spends three months in Haiti: March, April, and May of each year, with physicians going for approximately two-week visits in a rotating system. As one team leaves, another arrives. They are able to provide extensive eye care including examinations, surgery, and the fitting of glasses.

I was present once in Haiti when one of the groups was conducting eye examinations and performing surgery. The long lines of people waiting to be served were testimony to the care that was being given. I shall never forget seeing a man who stumbled to the clinic one day, hardly able to find his way. He had great difficulty opening and closing his eyes properly. After several hours in the clinic, he emerged able to see. He walked and shouted with great joy that his vision had been fully returned to him. What an amazing testimony that was to the wonderful concern and ministry of dedicated medical volunteers! Praise be to God!

Dr. Edward Hagan, a dentist from Sylvania, Georgia, and many others in his profession have shared their time and skills. Ed and his wife have often gone to Honduras, the Dominican Republic, and Haiti, spending a couple of weeks or so in rugged conditions performing dental services.

Dr. James Fields, a dermatologist from Nashville, Tennessee, and his wife, Linda, have been involved since 1984 in volunteer medical and educational work in St. Vincent, West Indies, providing more than forty-five thousand patient visits. Jim and Linda's love for the people of St. Vincent and devotion to their medical ministry are legendary across this Caribbean island. They have remained committed to such work every year, with teams of up to thirty or more participants coming from across the USA from Seattle to Boston, from Minnesota to Florida.

I asked Linda to share one of many moving stories of their ongoing relationship with one patient:

The darkness made it difficult to see the two women sitting in the doorway of their tiny house. One was a leprosy patient in her late sixties whose disease was no longer active; the other was her mother in her nineties. Because leprosy leaves hands and feet numb, patients frequently injure themselves without realizing it. After a bit of gentle persuasion the patient, whose hands revealed the ravages of her disease from earlier years, laboriously removed the long strip of cloth she had wrapped around her foot. Covering most of the sole of the foot was a large, badly infected ulcer, which had been there for more years than she could remember. The next day, Jim knelt on the floor and gently washed her feet. Then he and our daughter, Amy, now a pediatric nurse practitioner, made plaster molds of her feet, which were used to make custom sandals that would help heal the ulcer. The woman was provided with crutches, medicines, and instructions on how to care for her foot. Over a period of three years, the ulcer healed.

During this time, however, her crutches began to poke through the rotting floor of their little house, so she could no longer use them indoors. We asked one of our team members to tackle a rather unusual project. The little house was so wobbly that it needed stabilizing before re-flooring. Team member Ray Randolph, of Nashville, went to a man who makes concrete blocks. The curious blockmaker wanted to know why this stranger needed twenty-five blocks. When told why and for whom, the man gave the blocks and firmly refused any payment. As the blocks were being loaded onto the truck, Ray noticed that the blockmaker's small son had crossed eyes. Ray sent the family to the little hospital nearby, where the visiting UMVIM medical team included an ophthalmologist, Dr. Rowe Driver, also of Nashville. Dr. Driver operated on the child, straightening his eyes and changing his future.

With the aid of a borrowed truck jack, Ray raised the house, crawled underneath it and stabilized it with concrete block columns at each corner and in the middle. He then refloored it with wood from crates used by the team to ship an electronic organ they had brought to their host church that year. Enough wood was left over to replace the rusty tin door on the outside toilet, thus preventing possible injury to the elderly woman's numb hands. Part of the treatment to heal her ulcer involved daily soaks in a solution of vinegar and water. A church steward who twice each month delivered the vinegar and some groceries—provided by a church in South Carolina— came to know the two women whose house she had once avoided. She told Jim some time later, "You came not just to heal the sick, but to teach us how to love the unlovely."

A number of other teams, many of them composed of medical personnel, have returned to Haiti year after year to continue their ministry. For example, Alice and Bill White formerly of Charlotte, North Carolina, had their interest in Haiti aroused in 1979 and there was no turning back for them. As committed Christians with an interest in their church's mission outreach, they offered their large sailing boat to the Methodist Church of Haiti. After arrangements were completed for transfer of ownership, the Whites made the delivery, sailing the boat into Haitian waters.

Alice said:

We were touched by all that we saw and experienced. The human condition here was of an entire country in despair. We could not even stay in the boat because she floated in a harbor of sewage.

Bill felt there must be something we could do. I wasn't so sure, but in the winter of 1981 I started nursing school. Bill is a professional engineer with a great deal to offer. After a year, our home church, Providence United Methodist, sent a team with us to explore opportunities for a mission project. The church chose the Cap Haitian circuit for their ongoing international endeavor. In the ensuing years, Bill and volunteer teams, with funding from various churches, built five churches and two clinics, Tovar and Dondon, and drilled five water wells. During the mid eighties, as construction projects were completed, the focus began to shift from building teams to medical and surgical teams, mainly from the Western North Carolina Conference.

Since then, the two clinics, Tovar and Dondon, have provided medical care two or three times a year. The surgical team works at Hospital Bon Samaritain in Limbe with our team leader, Dr. Mike Barringer, spending six weeks there both in the fall and in the winter. Most recently, our project joined forces with the Development Program of L'Eglise Methodiste and opened a fully functioning community health center at the Tovar Clinic in 1997. This effort provides, for the first time, ongoing medical care to the people of that region with a Haitian staff supplemented by volunteer doctors, dentists, and nurses visiting three times a year.

It was intended from the beginning that this facility serve the community on a continuing basis, offering immunizations, prenatal care, and classes in hygiene and child care. Now the government insists that the service be maintained throughout the year, and to that we are committed, God willing and volunteers come forward. Cap Haitian is a particularly deprived area without any medical care other than this mission clinic.

I can still hear Dr. James T. McCord, an optometrist from the Tennessee Conference, telling a story from a mission experience in Panama. A local woman from an impoverished area was very distressed by her poor eyesight because she couldn't see well enough to teach her daughter the crafts that were essential to her future. Dr. McCord examined her eyes and fitted her with glasses that enabled her to see normally once again. A few days later her husband came to the clinic with a heavy stalk of bananas across his back. As he did not speak English, he spoke through an interpreter to explain who he was and why he had come. "I came to greet the doctor," he said, "and to thank you for the wonderful care you have given to my wife." The man was overcome with emotion, as was the doctor, as they embraced each other. Another life had just been changed.

Dr. Allen F. Delevett, a general practitioner from Brunswick, Georgia, has offered himself for medical service in several needy places. The first was Bolivia in response to a challenge received at the Medical Fellowship annual meeting. He and his wife were impressed by the "great corps of nurses and doctors at the Montero Methodist Hospital who were working under adverse conditions with joy, devotion, and love for the sick and financially deprived."

Another overseas assignment took Dr. Delevett and his wife to Zimbabwe. Dr. Rosalie Johnson, the missionary doctor at Old

Mutare Hospital, was due to go on furlough and had contacted the UMVIM office for a temporary replacement during her six-month leave. Dr. Delevett said:

> We had a rare opportunity to spend seven months in Zimbabwe, allowing Dr. Johnson to take a much-needed leave of absence and allowing Dorothy and me to work with the great Christian nurses and the many, many patients in the hospital and in the rural clinics. We worked harder than at any time since my internship in Baltimore. I was seventy-two when we were in Africa, and my fatigue at the end of each day was relieved by the next morning upon rising at five o'clock. I saw first-hand the promise of our Lord to those who wait upon him. He did renew my strength. I worked and did not faint. He cured my malaria in three days.

Dr. Delevett continued, "We have been blessed to go on mission trips to Jamaica with the Reverend George and Cora Herndon of the South Georgia Conference. Our church has supported us with prayers and gifts to mission. I also work part-time in a mental health clinic here in Brunswick."

Nurses have served on most medical teams and have provided valuable service as individual volunteers, serving several weeks or up to a year or longer. For example, Judy Neal, RN, of Kentucky, has worked with suffering and starving refugees in Burundi, Congo, Rwanda, and Uganda. She has returned with amazing stories of how God was able to use her and others to meet some of the desperate needs in those countries.

In the United States, the Red Bird Medical Center in Kentucky has received a host of medical personnel. The staff house on the Red Bird campus provides meals and a place for lodging. Nurse Nancie Allen of North Carolina is one of many who has had a fruitful ministry of caring and sharing at Red Bird. It is difficult, of course, to provide volunteer medical services in this country, even in needy communities, because of government and state regulations. Thus, most volunteers in medicine have had to serve abroad.

Several persons with emergency medical problems have been brought to this country for special treatment through the help of UMVIM personnel. To show how the system works, I received a call from Evans Bailey in Jamaica, telling me that a pastor in Haiti was suffering from an acute attack of kidney stones. He had flown to Jamaica seeking treatment, but none was available. It was then that Bailey called me. I immediately called Dr. George Evans in Dublin, Georgia. George is a veteran UMVIM participant and a certified urologist. He said to send the pastor on to Atlanta, that he would arrange transport to his clinic and return him home without charge, and this was done. Other similar stories come to mind as volunteers have reached out to help wherever possible in dealing with critical medical emergencies.

One of my special joys has been placing young pre-med students in mission service. These students come to us looking for an opportunity to serve in a mission hospital outside the United States. They know that in some situations they will be given an opportunity to learn much and to experience a wider range of medical work than they could do in this country. Two places have been used in particular. One is Jamaica, where several government medical centers have been open to us. The other is Kenya at the Maua Methodist Hospital. In both instances the local folks have been appreciative and always very supportive of young medical volunteers. The young people themselves have returned with tremendous optimism and excitement about possible future service as medical missionaries.

The UMVIM Medical Fellowship

The medical phase of UMVIM work has grown to such an extent that in 1989 the UMVIM Medical Fellowship was organized to provide leadership to the movement. Founders Dr. Michael Watson, Dr. William Spencer, Dr. James Fields and Linda Fields, Judy Neal, R.N., and Dr. Solomon Christian have laid a solid foundation for this medical ministry. Dr. Spencer was elected the first president. Membership is open to physicians, dentists, nurses, allied health professionals, clergy, and all who are interested in medical mission service. Its purpose is "to encourage its members and facilitate their expression of oneness in Jesus Christ, to answer the commandment that we love one another and to use their God-given skills and gifts to provide medical care and dental services in areas of special need." The current president of the UMVIM–SEJ

Medical Fellowship, which meets annually during the UMVIM rally weekend, is Dr. James Fields, a dermatologist from Nashville.

Dr. Watson and his wife, Mary Carolyn, produce *The Knock,* the medical bulletin of the Medical Fellowship. Under sponsorship of the UMVIM–SEJ board, the services of the Medical Fellowship and the bulletin are open to all persons anywhere with the same commitment to medical mission service. The medical and dental leaders listed above, plus a host of other practitioners and helpers, are at the forefront in extending this type of volunteer care throughout the world in the name of our denomination.

CHAPTER TEN

The Evangelistic and Christian Education Volunteers

Lord, speak to me, that I may speak in living echoes of thy tone;
as thou hast sought, so let me seek thine erring children lost and lone.

Frances R. Havergal, 1872 (Romans 14:7)

An emphasis on evangelism has always been central to the UMVIM ministry. Every team has an evangelistic purpose, even though the team's focus might be on medical or construction or technical work. Team members are expected to bear witness to their Christian faith in an appropriate manner. A number of evangelists have been placed as well, to conduct evangelistic efforts in full concert with local Methodist pastors and to lead seminars in evangelism for pastors and lay leaders. This work is undertaken at the invitation of the host churches and in response to negotiations that have been worked out in advance with the UMVIM office. Christian education and music teams have also been a strong part of the ministry.

Evangelistic teams are composed mainly of conference evangelists, pastors, and laity. The teams always have shared ministry and shared leadership. Both visiting evangelists and local people learn in the process, and all are expected to provide insights from their own experience and skills. Vacation Bible schools, although basically an American institution and not well-known outside the US, have become an important part of this ministry. Some teams have combined vacation Bible school with another project such as construction or building repair to help the local people meet an important community need. This dual approach can also be an opportunity to involve more local people.

A number of ministers have expressed interest in volunteering in English-speaking countries where they could participate actively in preaching services and other church events. The Reverend Dr. Douglas Newton of Panama City, Florida, saw UMVIM projects as opportunities to preach the gospel and share with the local people in practical ways. Doug led his first team to Dominica in 1979. He reports:

In the aftermath of Hurricane David, our ten-member team helped several families get a roof back on their homes. We worked, worshipped, laughed, and sang with the Methodists of Roseau. Our theme song was "I Can See Clearly Now the Rain Is Gone." I knew I was hooked on UMVIM when a little girl from one of the families we had helped to move back into their home thanked me with tears in her eyes, then held my hand to her lips in a tender kiss.

Dr. Newton's next place of service was Jamaica in a community known as Content, on the Manchester Circuit. The project was to help with building a new church. God opened new vistas in preaching and witnessing to the community. Doug wrote, "The experience of participating in the Wesley Church at Mandeville and the other churches on the circuit, preaching in open-air evangelistic services, seeing the completion of the minister's residence and the Content Church, have been some of the most fulfilling experiences of my life." He also reported, "We have seen four young American men answer the call of God to the ministry, serving with our teams in Jamaica." One of the favorite songs to come out of the UMVIM movement, "The Road to Mandeville," was written and often sung at the SEJ rallies by Doug and his wife, Gaynelle:

The road to Mandeville is in my memory still,
The lovely, lovely road to Mandeville.
From the Caribbean Sea to the flower laden hills,
It's a lovely, lovely road to Mandeville.

From old Montego Bay, we were singing all the way,
On the lovely, lovely road to Mandeville.
We went to spread good cheer, and serve the people there
When we traveled on the road to Mandeville.

From the plains of Sav-le-Mar to the mountain peaks afar,
It's a lovely, lovely road to Mandeville.
Through the Bamboo Avenue to the gorgeous mountain view,
It's a very lovely road to Mandeville.

They gave us love and care and joy while we were there,
In that lovely mountain place called Mandeville.
And when we said goodbyes, the tears were in our eyes
For the lovely, lovely folk of Mandeville.

The road to Mandeville is in my memory still,
The lovely, lovely road to Mandeville.

I think Doug's story is important to note. Here is a deeply committed evangelical pastor who got started with UMVIM through a disaster-relief project, then a new church building, and then he expanded that work to include a definite ministry of preaching and sharing of the Christian faith.

A similar story comes to mind of a retired minister and his wife, the Reverend George and Cora Herndon from the South Georgia Conference. These two have led well over a dozen teams to places in the Caribbean as well as to work sites here at home. Whatever the work project, they are always concerned about sharing the good news and letting the local people know why they have come. Whether conducting vacation Bible school, workshops, or retreats, their focus is on reaching children wherever they go to serve.

Back in the mid 1980s, Bishop Roberto Diaz of Costa Rica asked me to locate a Spanish-speaking pastor who could come and help in a national evangelistic campaign. I was fortunate that a college friend, the Reverend Ted Grout of the Rio Grande Conference, was willing to respond to this request. William Padilla, a layman from Ted's El Buen Samaritono United Methodist Church in Texas, also participated significantly in the campaign. Both being fluent in Spanish, their ministry was very effective.

A number of general evangelists of the church have been placed in preaching assignments as a part of the UMVIM movement; for example, Charles Dennis of the South Georgia Conference conducted evangelistic services and a seminar on the island of St. Kitts and was wonderfully received; the Reverend James Argue of Little Rock served in the Caribbean on a preaching mission; and the

Reverend Gale Wetzel from Kentucky has made frequent evangelistic trips to several countries.

Evangelistic work has been done by several retired pastors who have helped to supply vacancies for several months at a time. One is the Reverend Joseph Davis who, with his wife, Mary, served one of the family islands of the Bahamas.

In recent years a deliberate effort was begun in the Southeast to use volunteers in an evangelistic outreach among the deprived and marginalized people of our society. Two of the main leaders have been Mike Watson and Don Stewart, a lawyer from Anniston, Alabama. Dr. Watson points out, "It seems abundantly clear that the imperative of the early church was leading people to Christ, with major emphasis on those suffering with poverty. There are many thrilling accounts of the efforts of early Methodists who went to great lengths to preach the good news of salvation through Jesus Christ among the poor."

This concept is developed in *Taking the Church to the Unchurched: The Mission Cottage,* a booklet Dr. Watson has written. His belief is that volunteers can have a powerful influence working here at home in areas of desperate human need. The "mission cottage" is simply a place where folks can be invited to come to find friendship and, hopefully, to find Jesus Christ, from which may eventually come a new congregation. Already this is beginning to happen as Watson and Stewart give leadership. Watson firmly believes that "it is not enough to simply give money to the poor without personal involvement. We cannot depend on others to lead people to Christ. Problems do not disappear just because we throw money at them. The heart of the gospel is for every believer to share the good news of Jesus Christ."

The Oklahoma Conference under its UMVIM coordinator, the Reverend Larry Acton, is quite definite regarding its commitment to evangelism. Larry declares, "The purpose of Volunteers In Mission is to share the love of Jesus Christ in ways that make a Christian difference through participating in a mission opportunity. The place is not as important as the reality of serving people in a setting where a Christian difference is made. Volunteers seek to radiate the love of Jesus Christ, our wonderful Savior and Lord, while serving Him with gladness."

I believe everything we do in ministry is to honor Christ and to share our faith in an appropriate manner. Each of us can use our own skills and talents while at the same time being an invaluable witness to God's love and grace. That is why I believe UMVIM is practical Christianity at its finest!

CHAPTER ELEVEN

The Construction Volunteers

Take my life, and let it be consecrated, Lord, to thee.
Take my moments and my days; let them flow in ceaseless praise.
Take my hands, and let them move at the impulse of thy love.
Take my feet, and let them be swift and beautiful for thee.

Frances R. Havergal, 1873 (Romans 12:1)

The majority of UMVIM projects have been in the form of some type of construction or renovation of churches, parsonages, schools, social centers, or camps. The reason this type of service has become so popular is that almost anyone in reasonable health can participate, not necessarily needing to be a skilled worker. It is one practical way a person from almost any walk of life can offer willing hands to help. And their help can make a difference.

While it is true that most construction teams consist primarily of general helpers, it is always essential to have two or three skilled, experienced builders who know how to use the services of persons not familiar with the kind of work to be done. Many UMVIM teams have been blessed with talented, well-qualified builders who have shared their skills with many a beginner and their friendly, caring personalities with new friends in many countries. Supervising unskilled workers adds to a team leader's responsibility, but most seem to accept it without difficulty.

Two SEJ annual conferences have full-time coordinators to direct the work of volunteers on conference projects. The first was Western North Carolina Conference where the Reverend Joe Ervin was appointed construction coordinator several years ago. Since then, hundreds of thousands of dollars have been saved through the use of volunteer labor on new construction and repairs to church buildings. The same benefits have been achieved in the North Carolina Conference with Gary Smith as coordinator. The job of the coordinator requires much advance planning to select appropriate sites; locate and secure persons with the necessary skills and adequate funding; and supervise or arrange for supervision of the work, accommodations, and meals for the volunteers. In these two conferences, coordinating is a full-time job!

In Joe Ervin's case, he had developed a profound love for the Haitian people, who loved and respected him in return. As a leader of many conference teams to Haiti, he fast became known for his knowledge of the country and its people. Joe's bishop, L. Scott Allen, once asked why he did not do more mission work in his own conference. Joe responded, "Give me that job and I will gladly do so." The rest is history. His tireless schedule of work has enabled many new and renovated United Methodist properties to be completed, even as his eyesight has failed in recent years.

I count it one of my greatest privileges to have been a part of many of these teams, and in a few cases to have gone back later when the new or renovated facility was dedicated. On several such occasions, the resident bishop of the sponsoring conference has been present to share in the celebrations. This happened when Bishop C. P. Minnick, Jr, episcopal leader of North Carolina Conference, accompanied project coordinator Annette Bingham and other team members to Jamaica for the dedication and opening of a large new social center in one of Kingston's most depressed areas. It was a time of great celebration. The Governor General of Jamaica gave the principal address. Bishop Minnick in his remarks mentioned that more than eighty persons from North Carolina had had the privilege of sharing in construction of this important Christian activity center.

Another major church building project was completed in Costa Rica, thanks to nearly a dozen teams from the former Louisville Conference. Bishop Paul Duffey encouraged these groups, and he returned with some of the team members for the dedication services. Warm relationships established during the project helped cement ties between the local churches and the volunteers.

From South Georgia, a dozen teams went to Belize to help construct the new Lake Independence Church (its name later changed to St. Luke Church), one of their most important projects. Bishop Richard C. Looney participated in the final days of the work (his height was helpful in reaching into difficult areas for the last bit of painting).

One of the first episcopal visits to an UMVIM construction project, of which I am aware, was made by Bishop Frank L. Robertson of the Louisville Area, who joined with team members in Kingston in renovating Saxthorpe House, headquarters of the Methodist Church's Jamaica District. From the North Central Jurisdiction, Bishop R. Sheldon Duecker has promoted and participated in overseas work/study trips. Bishop Felton E. May of the Northeastern Jurisdiction has worked with volunteers serving in emergency situations in several African countries, especially those burdened with heavy relief responsibilities. Other bishops and conference mission leaders have provided similar support to many teams.

Presiding Bishop Mvume Dandala of the Methodist Church of Southern Africa has written a letter to express his thanks for the teams that have visited his area. He wrote, "You don't come to do mission for us, but with us. You've put dignity into our work by being willing to take up a hammer and saw or physician's instrument yourselves and do the actual hard labor with us. You have been able to sanctify labor in the process."

Construction projects often form bonds that endure. And a bishop going to participate in volunteer mission activity strengthens the bonds. It sends a strong message to volunteers and hosts alike that the construction project is important and the personal relationships formed by working together as Christian friends will not be forgotten. We did it together!

CHAPTER TWELVE

Service by Age Groups

*Jesus said to them again, "Peace
be with you. As the Father has
sent me, so I send you."*

John 20:21

While it is true that most volunteers serve as members of a construction or medical team, many do so as partners with those of a similar age group. That does not mean that teams are segregated on the basis of age, but it does mean that certain groups find it easier to organize around schools or college or on some other basis.

Young adult and college-age young people as well as chaperoned high-school student groups are quite active in the movement, especially during the summertime. Teams are usually organized primarily from one college campus, but with invitations to a limited number of other participants. Campus ministers across the country cite the incredible learning experiences and change of lifestyle by their volunteers. Their hosts are also usually quite affirming of the teams.

I want to point out the work being done by the United Methodist chaplain at DePauw University as an example of some of the outstanding and creative service being rendered by DePauw students. The Reverend Dr. Fred Lamar has been most meticulous in dealing with highly sensitive, intercultural relationships. His emphasis is directed primarily toward building personal relationships, taking time to be with the people, having fun with them, and sharing in moments of deep reflection.

Dr. Lamar began taking groups in 1976 to such places as Dulac Clinic in Louisiana; Guatemala; Honduras; Haiti; Panama; Peru;

Jamaica; Mexico; and Americus, Georgia, housing. His work grew to include projects in Calcutta, Costa Rica, Colombia, Maine cooperative factory, Kenya, Sierra Leone, Nicaragua, Philippines, Florida housing, China, US Virgin Islands hurricane repair, Brazil, Mississippi housing, Kentucky housing, the Dominican Republic, Indiana housing, El Salvador, South Carolina housing, Ecuador, Argentina, and Bosnia refugee children. From its beginning with two teams per year, this quickly increased to an annual average of four teams.

One country in which these college students served and grew was Bosnia, and I think it deserves special attention. Preparations were made far in advance and were extremely thorough, necessary in view of the security situation in the country. Three collective housing centers were established to help children adapt to a new community and to offer their families a way to provide some "normal activity." Program activities are led by refugees or displaced young women who receive training from the program manager and psychologist. Fred reports that the place where his team of twelve persons worked at Travnik was a Muslim enclave, and most of the sixteen hundred refugee children at the Youth House were Muslims. All were victims of the war, and all equally in need of love. We challenged our group to practice a ministry of "hanging out."

In trying to create a relaxed atmosphere so trust and hope could develop, Dr. Lamar had his team involved in simple play with the children. "We blew bubbles, played basketball, helped in English classes, walked downtown to see the spot where Grandmama was buying bread when the big bomb fell—after which 'we never saw her again.' While this was going on, other volunteers were at work on construction projects, and each complemented the other form of ministry." In conclusion, he stated that, "We kept asking the same question: What does it mean to live for Christ and like Christ with a people who have been raped and slaughtered in our Lord's name? (The high-school teachers were amazed to see so much good coming from Christians. They had thought Christians were generous only with their artillery and grenades.) They wanted to know more about Methodism, so a class was arranged for this purpose. In answer to my question above, we decided that it meant hammers and nails, shovels and sweat, and love and time to listen to the little children."

Bishop R. Sheldon Duecker of Indiana has said:

We talk about being a global church, but we do not provide much hands-on experience for youth and young adults except for what a few of our colleges are doing. In 1989 I was leading a group from Northern Illinois to Mozambique and Zimbabwe. While we were delayed in Zambia, we met a group of Presbyterian youth from the USA who were in Africa on a work camp. The conversation with them led me to determine to do something for United Methodist youth. When I returned home, I called the Boards of Global Ministries and Discipleship to inquire whether there were any denominational programs of this nature. The answer in both cases was "No, but it is something we should look into." Since I was the liaison bishop to the North Central Jurisdiction UMVIM group, I shared that concern, and they were excited with the prospect and decided to take on the sponsorship.

Later we worked and worshiped with twelve young people from the Zimbabwe Conference under the direction of a Zimbabwean, lived in their homes and shared their food. From my perspective, I have observed that this experience has changed lives. Some said it was the highlight of their life, and others have entered church-related vocations. The Zimbabwe youth made a great contribution to us. Our youth were at a loss to select hymns, to offer prayer, or to use the Bible. Their young people had a much better command of these resources of the faith. It was a humbling but enriching time for our group.

Quite often a Sunday school class of young adults (including but not limited to college students) decide they want to take on a mission project. Usually the assignment is made in connection with the school situation in which they will be visiting, such as classes in music, drama, and recreational activities. The mutual exchange of personnel with local young adults and their families has led to much deeper understandings of one another and appreciation for the other's culture.

Another age-group active in this movement is older persons and retirees. Many of these folks can serve for extended periods, given the necessary support. They have been occupied in a wide variety of services such as counseling, teaching, practicing medicine, assisting in church offices, and providing technical assistance and advice. Many institutions of our church in this country would probably have to close their doors if it were not for the thousands of older volunteers who come on a regular basis week after week. A much smaller number serve beyond our shores, and they are equally welcomed by their hosts.

Quite a number of retired United Methodist missionaries have returned as volunteers to their earlier place of assignment. John and Ruth Shryock of Arizona have made several trips back to Zimbabwe and Mozambique. John has been working with the financial offices and Ruth in medical services, both providing much-needed help in their fields for a number of months at a time. Dr. Don Rudy of Minnesota has returned to Zimbabwe and also to Kenya for several months on each trip to help staff church hospitals. Lloyd and Margaret Schaad of Washington have traveled to Mozambique and Angola, he to work in agricultural programs and she in hospitals. John and Ruth Schevenius of Minnesota have gone back to Zimbabwe to serve, he as an engineering advisor after the war to advise on priority projects for electrical and other services disrupted by the conflict. Ruth has been involved in several plans to help with home industries. Ken and Iweeta McIntosh of Texas have returned to Hong Kong to continue their ministry as volunteers. Doubtless there are many other traditional missionaries who have joined the ranks as Volunteers In Mission, as people who have much to offer, even on a time-limited basis.

So people from nearly all age groups can participate if in reasonably good health. The older folk can often give much longer periods of service, up to one or more years, as they do not usually have the same time constraints. Older people also have invaluable skills and talents developed over a lifetime. Likewise, younger people can offer their enthusiasm and zeal as well as their skills and special gifts.

CHAPTER THIRTEEN

Across America

Reports from the Five Jurisdictions, the General Board of Global Ministries, Ecumenical Partners, and Disaster Response

Praise to the Lord, who doth prosper thy work and defend thee;
surely his goodness and mercy here daily attend thee.
Ponder anew what the Almighty can do, who with his love doth
*   befriend thee.*

Joachim Neander, 1680

This chapter will focus on the growth and development of the UMVIM movement in the five jurisdictions of The United Methodist Church in this country. Brief accounts are also included of UMVIM involvement with the General Board of Global Ministries, with UMCOR and disaster relief, and with ecumenical partners.

Information has come chiefly from UMVIM coordinators in each jurisdiction with input also from team leaders and volunteers who have shared their stories with me. While not intended to be comprehensive reports, their stories illustrate how UMVIM has been blessed of God and continues to grow across the entire church and further afield.

North Central Jurisdiction (NCJ)

The Volunteers In Mission movement was begun in the NCJ, under another name, in 1980 by Carl Walker, a layman in the West Michigan Conference. Carl was a successful businessman in

Kalamazoo who at age forty-four began contemplating his life and future. This led him to offer his skill as a pilot for mission work in the West African country of Liberia, where remote villages and mission stations are perilously isolated. Carl has said, "The work I did in Liberia was the most rewarding experience I've ever had."

Intersharing. Carl returned to Michigan and founded Intersharing, an organization to help dedicated laypersons with special skills to find a place of service where their talents and their love could help enrich the lives of others. In 1989, Beverly Nolte was named the NCJ Coordinator, replacing Joseph Wagner who followed Walker. By 1996, after more than a decade of volunteer mission activity, the Intersharing board decided to use the UMVIM logo and voted to change its name to UMVIM-NCJ.

Nomads. In this program, initiated by Hawley and Dorothy Fabrick of Illinois, people with recreational vehicles offer skills for work projects at local churches, mission agencies, camps, children's homes, and so forth, providing their own transportation and housing. Nomads also work in disaster response across the United States. Most projects are scheduled from January to April each year, with a growing number in the fall. The initial group of Nomads in 1988 numbered twenty couples with three work projects. By 1995 about five hundred participants were involved. A growing number of single persons participate. The program has increased 35 percent since 1994.

Mission Discovery Program. Upon the urging of Bishop Sheldon Duecker, the Intersharing board organized Mission Discovery in 1992 to involve youth between the ages of sixteen and twenty-six in overseas work or study trips. Evelyn Taylor Cain, a former missionary to Brazil and NCJ missionary in residence, coordinated the first overseas trip to Zimbabwe with twenty-two youth participants. In 1993 eighteen youth and young adults went to San Juan, Puerto Rico. In 1995 fifteen youth participants and three adult leaders went to Manila. A reverse Mission Discovery event brought youth from three overseas host countries to Chicago for a work/study experience in June 1996.

Operation Classroom. This is one of the largest volunteer ministries in the NCJ and was started about 1986, under the leadership of the Reverend Joseph Wagner, to upgrade classroom buildings in

Sierra Leone and Liberia. Many work teams were sent by the North Indiana and South Indiana Conferences until the political situation made it unsafe for individuals or groups to travel in West Africa. The emphasis shifted to home-mission projects where Fred Payne, a South Indiana Conference contractor by trade, was working with volunteers repairing and constructing new church furnishings on US projects, mainly in-conference ones. Their efforts have allowed many persons to offer their time and skills, saving the conference approximately $2,000,000 over the years.

Building a Church. The Reverend Jack D. Travelstead, retired and now living in Springfield, Illinois, recalls being asked by the Reverend Alain Rocourt of Haiti to assist in building a church for a new congregation in the community of Furcy, Haiti. Jack gets stirred up as he tells the story:

> When it was time to begin, we traveled there with excitement. The site was one-and-a-half miles beyond the end of the road. We took the building materials in by hand. With our new Haitian friends we laid blocks, poured cement, painted walls, built the pews. We manufactured some tools—adding a bamboo pole to the paint roller handle—and the local women carried water for mortar and cement. When it was finished, the team from Haiti and Illinois was proud to have worked together on a holy place. The white church is visible from all around the surrounding mountains. It is truly the center of the community.
>
> Daniel Isador, one of two agronomists in the area, helped educate peasant farmers there in growing vegetables for their families and for sale at market. He taught them to build rows of retaining walls on the mountainsides to prevent soil erosion. Soon the mountains were covered with beautiful, edible plants. Death from starvation was soon a thing of the past in that rural village.

Building a School. The community then asked for help in building a school for their children. Teams rose to the occasion and built eight classrooms. After this the people said, "The church has taught us to farm and we no longer die from starvation. Now the church is teaching our children. Shouldn't we learn more about the church? Perhaps we will turn from voodoo and its superstition." And so the teams gladly responded.

"And what happened to us?" Jack asked. "During those months, I preached no sermons on missions! Our people told their own stories! Our people were changed. Giving to all causes increased. Team members wanted to know how they could serve our local church better. Other mission projects soon followed. We can bring a new quality of life to a people!"

Rebuilding. Wes Loving, an electrical contractor from New Berlin, Wisconsin, contacted the UMVIM office in Atlanta in 1981 when only the Southeastern Jurisdiction had an UMVIM office. Wes was interested in doing voluntary mission service. We put him in touch with team leaders Norris Allen and Glenn Abernathy of the Tennessee Conference, who were about to leave on a trip to the island of Dominica in the West Indies. They invited Wes to join their team in rebuilding a burned church at Layou. The experience was life-changing for him. The next year he went again with the same leaders to work on repairing hurricane-damaged Wesley High School, also on Dominica, and joined them again in 1984 to investigate future work opportunities on St. Vincent. Wes had all along wanted to organize volunteers in his own Wisconsin Conference. He and a colleague, Harriett Young, realized they needed help in coordinating the growing number of volunteers; so they organized a Wisconsin Conference UMVIM Committee, which now has sent teams to Grenada, Costa Rica, Trinidad, Sierra Leone, Bolivia, Brazil, Montserrat, and to Africa University in Zimbabwe. Early in 1998 when on a visitation mission to Brazil investigating sites for future teams, Wes died suddenly of a heart attack. But he leaves behind a legacy of love and devotion to Christian mission. In this connection, I am aware of four volunteers who were busy serving the Lord at the time of their deaths while in mission service—one in Florida after Hurricane Andrew, one in Mexico, one in Grenada, and now Wes. All died of natural causes. Their respective conferences have established UMVIM memorials in their memory.

Following a Mission Saturation event in the Des Moines District of Iowa Conference, a Panamanian speaker challenged the attendees to come to Panama to help the church there with construction projects. A nineteen-member team from Des Moines District went to work at Puerto Armuelles in January 1986. This was followed by numerous international work teams and hundreds of youths traveling throughout the USA each summer. During the great flood of 1993, the Iowa Conference received dozens of work teams from other states. They learned how to receive as well as how to give.

From Minnesota, retired missionary engineer John Schevenius reported on a number of individual mission trips he has made back to Zimbabwe, sometimes accompanied by his wife, Ruth, who is a microbiologist. Their trips began in 1980 when John was asked to return to evaluate the war damage and make estimates of reconstruction costs for church property. He said, "This was a great experience for Ruth and me in so many ways. I felt able to give some reasonably accurate estimates and the priority guidelines for rebuilding, and dealt with some infrastructure problems." Peanut butter is an important staple in the local diet in Zimbabwe. Ruth is a charter member of Compatible Technology (CTI), a nonprofit, para-church group in Minnesota that develops post-harvest technology for underdeveloped areas of the world. John and Ruth, with their colleagues at CTI, developed a food grinder at very reasonable cost, and with the help of the University of Zimbabwe introduced the product to the country. The grinders are now provided in Zimbabwe, where they form the basis of a cottage industry for women's cooperatives.

Heifer Project International. One of the most ambitious efforts of UMVIM-NCJ has come from the Iowa Conference, where Bill and Dorothy Appelgate have promoted a continuing drive on behalf of the Heifer Project.

The RX ConneXion. Another development has been the establishment of the RX ConneXion, a channel through which medical personnel may offer to serve. The present focus is on the island of Jamaica in cooperation with the medical committee of the Jamaica District of the Methodist Church. The latter has been in operation for a number of years placing volunteers in strategic parts of the country.

Northeastern Jurisdiction (NEJ)

United Methodism in the Northeast does not have a formal jurisdictional structure, so the College of Bishops names UMVIM coordinators for the jurisdiction. All volunteer mission work takes place in and through local churches and annual conferences. The

Eastern Pennsylvania Conference has had several coordinators who over the years have provided key leadership in deploying volunteer teams, especially to Puerto Rico, under episcopal leadership of the Philadelphia Area.

The twelve annual conferences of this region have modest program units for a few special programs of a jurisdictional nature. Before 1996, a $2,000 annual appropriation was made for the office of a part-time volunteer coordinator. The jurisdiction increased the appropriation to $6,000 for the 1997–2000 quadrennium.

UMVIM, first begun as an organized movement in the Southeastern Jurisdiction, was the model for the Northeast under the leadership of retired college professor Dr. Earl Griswold and his wife, Lura, also known as "Sunny," who had engaged college students in mission trips for many years. Soon after the 1980 General Conference affirmed the UMVIM movement, the Griswolds volunteered and were appointed by Bishop James K. Mathews of the Washington Area to serve as the first NEJ coordinators.

Dr. Griswold and Sunny continued their intensive service throughout the eighties. One day in 1990, after completing a long day of packing blankets and clothing for shipment to Russia, Dr. Griswold went home and died in his sleep. He had given the last full measure of his devotion to the needs of suffering humanity. Until mid 1992, Sunny Griswold very effectively continued the mission and ministry that she and her husband had shared.

In 1992 at the NEJ Conference, the Reverend Kenneth S. Jones was selected as the first formally designated jurisdictional coordinator. He was reelected by the NEJ College of Bishops in 1996. When Ken began his duties, he received a checkbook balance of some $1,300 and copies of a work-team handbook. Prior to 1992 there was no documentation of persons, teams, or destinations, but plenty of folklore concerning teams traveling across the world. Several conferences have held their own VIM rallies since 1992. Annual gatherings of all conference VIM coordinators have also been held. The first-ever VIM-NEJ rally was held at Camp Casowasco, New York, in October 1996.

During his first quadrennium, Ken Jones organized NEJ teams to Jamaica, Russia, Africa University twice, Mississippi flood relief, and to the Warren Village Housing Project in Denver at the time of the General Conference. The UMVIM-NEJ coordinator is Gregory Forrester of New York.

One active team organizer is the Reverend Tom Clark of the West Virginia Conference. He contacted the UMVIM–SEJ office a number of years ago and was given help in starting out with his first team. Now Tom has led groups to Mexico, Jamaica, Nicaragua, Russia, and Costa Rica, as well as to Africa University in Zimbabwe.

Janice and John Cogswell, formerly of Massachusetts, have participated on fifty-nine work teams and led more than fifty of them. Their present project is helping provide furniture for the Kusayapu Institute in Chile.

Mat Merker, a psychiatric nurse from Maryland, has actively recruited volunteers and organized teams from across the state. She is well-qualified to lead diverse groups that have gone to critical areas of need at home and abroad.

Perhaps it is fitting to complete this report on the Northeast with a statement sent to me by Bishop S. Clifton Ives of the West Virginia Area. He wrote:

While in my first pastoral appointment in the 1960s, I wrote to the Board of Missions suggesting that mission interpretation could be increased by giving laypersons a one- or two-week experience at a mission site. I was informed that such would not be possible since there was a process all missionaries needed to go through before going to the mission field.

In 1992, I was elected to the episcopacy and assigned to West Virginia. Early on, it became evident that West Virginia had become the recipient of many teams of Volunteers In Mission, and we were blessed each year to be able to host persons from around the world who came to help us. But West Virginians were already engaged through sending teams to the Caribbean and Mexico. I gave strong affirmation to what was happening and encouraged the conference to intensify its volunteer efforts. During my first quadrennium, I went with a team to Russia. Teams from our conference have followed every year since. In 1997 I accompanied one of several conference teams to Africa University. At our annual conference in 1997 we commissioned and recognized over one hundred people who would be Volunteers In Mission that year.

South Central Jurisdiction (SCJ)

Dr. Kenneth McIntosh, SCJ field representative for the General Board of Global Ministries, called together several groups in the late 1970s to talk about ways of promoting the volunteer mission movement in the region. I was invited to these discussions, served as a consultant, and shared the story of how this ministry had started in the Southeast. At that time, the UMVIM office in Atlanta received many calls for assistance by people in the SCJ wanting information about mission placements.

Four strong pastors in the SCJ who were early pioneers of the volunteer movement were Melvin West of Missouri, James Palmer and Cliff Lamb of Texas, and Larry Eisenberg of Oklahoma. Larry's volunteer service reached back to the Caravan movement of the forties. The first coordinator named by the SCJ College of Bishops was the Reverend Hans Aurbakken, a former missionary to Africa. He was succeeded by Jo Ann Small, who was followed by the Reverend Max Marble, son of missionaries to India. Max began his work in 1988, serving until 1992 as the only full-time coordinator for the jurisdiction. He helped establish and provide training for coordinators in all of the annual conferences, linked together a network of more than thirty-five hundred volunteers, developed a quarterly newspaper; and his office provided a complete and up-to-date listing of teams and mission opportunities. Despite a recommendation from the Jurisdictional Committee on Finance and Administration for a 20 percent increase in the budget, the office was voted out of existence by the jurisdiction's Executive Committee. This decision reduced the staff coordinator position to part-time. Ray Branton, who also served as the SCJ executive director, filled the position, assisted by two part-time secretaries. At his retirement in 1998 a new director, Dr. Thalia Matherson, replaced Branton.

In the early 1990s, the Oklahoma Conference under the leadership of Bishop Dan E. Solomon established a full-time position of conference coordinator and named the Reverend Larry Acton to that post. (This was the first time for such an appointment in coordinating all UMVIM activities of any conference. However, Western North Carolina and North Carolina Conferences have had full-time coordinators for in-conference projects for a number of years.) Acton's office is serving as a coordination point for several major disaster relief and other type ministries. The coordinator's office sponsors a biannual rally that draws up to seven hundred participants and serves as a referral point for several national and international projects.

In Oklahoma, Tulsa First Church has been one of the most active churches in the UMVIM ministry. Since 1983, Tulsa First has sent volunteer teams and individuals to Uganda, Jamaica, Mexico, Costa Rica, Oklahoma Indian Missionary Conference, Bolivia, Russia, Cuba, Estonia, Ghana, Israel, and Mount Sequoah, Arkansas, with many projects receiving repeated visits. Its ministries have included construction, medical, evangelistic, and Christian-education workers.

The South Central Jurisdiction is home to many of the historic national mission agencies of our denomination. One example is McCurdy School in Española, New Mexico, ministering to a predominantly Hispanic population where community tension often runs high. Dee Dee Heffner, director of church relations, said, "McCurdy School could not have the outreach that it does without our current Volunteers In Mission program. They serve throughout the year, with a major increase in the summer months to help with special programs such as camps. The most important aspect of the service is its impact on the lives of children and young people as they share their witness for Jesus Christ."

The Office of Creative Ministries under the Reverend Melvin E. West of Missouri has developed the Festival of Sharing, a gathering of people and goods that seeks to respond to the effects of hunger, poverty, injustice, and crisis. It is an ecumenical venture with many denominations cooperating and providing service for hundreds of volunteers. "United Methodists responded with typical enthusiasm to the nineteenth annual ingathering," according to a report in the *Arkansas United Methodist*:

> From every corner of the state they came, in cars, trucks, vans, and by the trailer-full. For hours on the morning of November 23, 1996, the street in front of First United Methodist of Little Rock was jammed with vehicles and volunteers loading tons of

relief goods—from blankets and cooking utensils to medicines and school supplies—onto two large transport trucks for distribution by Church World Service around the world and for agencies in the state.

"Operacion Hagar" is a program for building houses for the indigent population in the barrios of Juarez, Mexico, and is sponsored by the UMVIM-SCJ and UMCOR. More than two thousand volunteers from across the nation have constructed over two hundred houses for the working poor just across the border.

The Sager Brown Center for Enabling Ministries in Baldwin, Louisiana, is perhaps the largest new institution to be formed directly out of mission services by volunteers. This facility was used in coordinating disaster-relief efforts in the wake of Hurricane Andrew after the floods in the Midwest. It has now expanded to provide a wide variety of community services, such as a computer literacy program, nurse training, and a poultry project. The center receives volunteers who assist in the teaching programs, home building, and library development. A large warehouse related to UMCOR stockpiles items for disaster-response distribution as needed at home and abroad. It is staffed primarily by volunteers. During recent years of flooding, this region of the church has hosted hundreds of teams from across the country. More than five hundred teams have served in Missouri and Iowa alone. The United Methodist Church is always committed to the long haul, which means volunteers will be needed far into the future.

Marking another first for the South Central region, the Central Texas Conference in 1995 held an UMVIM service before annual conference, led by Bishop Joe Wilson and the conference cabinet. More than four hundred persons preregistered for this unique experience.

In 1997 still another exciting first was taking place as an SCJ team was in ministry with the Methodist Church in Hong Kong under the leadership of Ken and Iweeta McIntosh. Having served there earlier as missionaries, Ken and Iweeta were right at home. Plans are underway for future teams to this important gateway to that part of the world.

Western Jurisdiction (WJ)

The first Volunteers In Mission coordinator in this region was Ann Langer of Boulder, Colorado. She began in 1986 and served until 1991 on a voluntary basis. Ann was an enthusiastic supporter of this ministry and faithful in her attendance at various national volunteer events. As this jurisdiction has no mission structure other than the College of Bishops and the annual conferences, she had difficulty in establishing her work across the geographically widest jurisdiction in our denomination. She worked primarily through conference coordinators and their committees.

The next and present coordinator is Blythe Stanton of Greenbank, Washington. Like her predecessor, she is a volunteer, serving that vast area with very limited financial resources. Blythe said:

My role as coordinator is to keep the conference coordinators informed about places for volunteers to serve; acquainting them with materials that would be helpful in training, publicity, and communication; and assisting them by suggesting ways for churches and agencies in their conferences to prepare for receiving volunteers.

The excitement for the movement is contagious. Individuals and churches are full of enthusiasm at the idea of this personal Christian service. Their eagerness to get going needs to be tempered with attention to what can seem to be picky details. Striking a balance between enthusiasm and quality control is a tension that I believe will always exist in this grassroots movement. Our conference coordinators meet together annually so they can interact with each other and share ideas and problems. One team member said, "It was a spiritual growth experience disguised as work!"

The Alaska Missionary Conference in this jurisdiction has received many teams over the years. They come from all over the country to help on church building projects, summer camp programs, and a variety of ministries. Glide Memorial Church in San Francisco is an example of how a large, central-city church can host many volunteers. Often these helpers assist in Glide's huge daily food program.

At the 1996 General Conference in Denver, more than three hundred volunteers labored at a number of churches and agencies in the area during those two weeks, building and dedicating a Habitat for Humanity house. Two young volunteers from Alaska, Verda Carey and Claudette Curtis, said of their experience with the Denver project, "We wonder why we waited so long to work as Volunteers In Mission!"

California-Pacific coordinator Don Sparling is full of praise for the many volunteers who have come to that area to assist in disaster relief. Volunteer Cheryl Reeder from Lock Haven, Pennsylvania, wrote:

> One of my first lessons to learn in California was that a victim is a victim regardless of the severity or type of disaster. Again, I discovered that the ministry was not so much the task as it was the people for whom the tasks were being completed. I was disheartened with the media. Why didn't they tell us about the victims who still, after one full year, do not have comfortable beds of their own? I found myself in a neighborhood suffering heavy earthquake damage, yet the lawns held beautiful citrus trees, which to me became a sign of hope.

Cheryl concluded with thanks to her home support group and all those from whom she came. "I learned there is not blind faith. Just faith."

The Reverend David Wolf, VIM coordinator for the California-Nevada Conference, and Dr. Norman Eade led a strong team to Central Russia in 1994. They wrote:

> We were struck by the obvious poverty of the area and the antiquated farm methods being used. The houses we were there to help build were small, with simple construction. We were able to see firsthand some of the problems facing the Russian people. At first, the people were reserved and not sure what to expect from us. After seeing us work on their houses, however, they became more friendly. Our two-week assignment may have had just a small impact on one village. But if this happens in other places and often enough, it can make a positive impression and encourage an otherwise depressed population to rebuild their country.

Zeda Wall Dudley of Powell, Wyoming, illustrates some of the fine service being rendered by individual volunteers. While she was needing a break from caring for her elderly mother, an unexpected invitation to go on a mission team to the Caribbean seemed to provide just the answer. She and Amy Jacobs, both from the Yellowstone Conference, have served together in a number of overseas areas. On three occasions Zeda, a retired schoolteacher, found herself in potentially dangerous situations. In St. Vincent, she said:

> I witnessed a drug delivery on an isolated beach. Another time, in Bolivia, I was with a group travelling in a car that was struck by a bus. The third time, I was in La Paz when the military police fired tear gas into a group of striking rural schoolteachers. Fortunately, I was not harmed. I have had hugs and Christian love shown to me by people of many countries, cultures, and colors. I wouldn't trade one minute of my experiences for any amount of money. You just can't imagine the joy and filling of the spirit that you will experience until you have actually gone on a VIM trip. In fact, I am typing this out in a hurry so I can go to Billings, Montana, to catch a plane on the way to St. Maarten to help repair houses damaged in the last hurricane.

Her story reminds me, thankfully, that there have been only a few serious accidents or emergencies in this ministry over many years. Once, a bus loaded with volunteers from Western North Carolina was detained in Guatemala by a group of bandits. This situation turned quite serious, but no one was harmed. On another occasion, a small plane loaded with North Georgia volunteers had to make a forced landing in a pineapple field in Honduras. In Jamaica, a group of bandits threatened a team from Mississippi, but left without incident. There have been several fatalities; however, all have been due to natural causes.

An innovation for this jurisdiction has been the development in the California-Nevada Conference of Care-a-Vanners, a program for folks with RVs to work and take their mobile homes with them. Oregon-Idaho has sent a series of youth teams to prepare meals and meet people at the Glide Memorial Church, with hopes that leadership will develop from those participants. Alaska and Yellowstone have had the challenge of hosting many teams, yet have sent teams and individuals to other places. Churches in the California-Pacific, Desert Southwest, and Pacific Northwest

Conferences have continuing relationships with overseas areas and regularly send teams there.

After a major fire in Alaska destroyed several hundred homes, volunteers are helping families to rebuild. After heavy flooding in the Pacific Northwest, severe damage still awaits attention from construction crews.

From Sacramento, Dorothy Miller and Jane Henderson shared a bit of the excitement of a team from St. Mark Church, which has gone twice to Mexico:

> Soon after arriving in Mexico, any one of us who thought we were going on a vacation either gave up those thoughts or drastically changed our ideas of what a vacation was supposed to be. But soon, neither the threat of scorpions, crowded traveling conditions, limited and regulated use of bathroom facilities, nor the threat of 120-degree temperatures could dampen the spirits of the team. Our work was in support of the Heifer Project at Tlancualpican where Terry and Muriel Henderson have served for many years in an agricultural training ministry for peasants who try to survive on very poor soil. The lives of many rural Mexican families are being improved through their own efforts of applying the skills being offered by the Hendersons with the aid of VIM teams.

One other account from Dorothy Miller concerns her group's outreach to Native Americans. She reported:

> Each summer, United Methodist high-school youth volunteer to spend a week on an Indian reservation to help weatherize houses—repairing roofs, building new porches, installing windows, replacing worn siding, updating plumbing, painting, etc. Preparation for team membership requires the group to raise funds to pay for transportation, food, and materials needed for the project. Youth teams from several congregations convene and plan their work together. Cherished friendships are made that can last a lifetime.
>
> Each year it is thrilling to hear the young people witness to their faith and how their lives have been changed. They express feelings of pride from learning new skills, of accomplishment from having helped some less-fortunate family, of exaltation from just plain fun, a sense of appreciation to their home

congregation for having supported their fund-raising efforts, and above all, a great warmth and satisfaction that comes from putting their Christian faith into action.

The Reverend David Blackburn, a former field representative of GBGM, recalled much activity at home and abroad by teams from the Western Jurisdiction, particularly to neighboring Mexico. According to Mexican leader the Reverend Galal Gough, "In 1965 what was originally called the Joint Commission for Church Extension in Mexico was founded by the Southern California-Arizona Conference." Gough is president of the Joint Commission. This group was first organized at the suggestion of Mexican Bishop Alejandro Ruiz, who felt that certain churches received a disproportionate amount of assistance while others had little or no help at all. Sending volunteer teams has been a major part of this effort from the beginning, with other features being added. "To reflect a more progressive philosophy of cooperative mission, its name has been changed to The United Methodist Joint Commission for Cooperation and Church Extension between Mexico and the United States," said Gough.

Southeastern Jurisdiction (SEJ)

Much of the information and illustrations about UMVIM in the Southeast is covered in the text itself as UMVIM's story unfolded. Nine southern states with fourteen annual conferences make up this section of The United Methodist Church. A number of SEJ conferences were active in volunteer ministry several years before UMVIM itself was organized in 1976. The most active conferences were Florida, Western North Carolina, South Carolina, and Holston. Several others developed programs on a smaller scale. In all cases, enthusiastic and committed laypersons and ministers teamed up to share ideas and strategy.

Alabama/West Florida Conference

The Reverend Dr. Lester Spencer, Jr., is a long-time UMVIM participant who received his first taste of hands-on ministry through

UMVIM in 1978. He was the leader of an Auburn University student team to Belize that provided his initial experience. While a student at Candler School of Theology, he served one summer as coordinator of teams for the Methodist Church of Mexico, and has since taken teams to many countries. In 1994 Spencer was asked to lead an investigative team from the SEJ for consultations with the Methodist Church of Cuba, which opened up that country to groups from across the United States. Extensive video documentaries were made to assist in the preparation of future teams to Cuba. Spencer currently serves as vice-president of the UMVIM-SEJ board.

For many years, the Reverend Ted Hoagland provided vital leadership to the developing conference program. He has specialized in Costa Rica, Mexico, and Guatemala. Leaders of the effort to build parsonages in low-income areas are Jimmy Scruggs and Rudy Heintzelman. The Reverend Donald Brill, conference mission secretary, inspired many congregations and individuals to serve with UMVIM. In 1998 the conference established a Brill Memorial Scholarship Fund in his memory to assist individuals who want to serve, but have limited resources.

Another pastor in this conference vitally involved with UMVIM is the Reverend Dr. Douglas Newton:

> My involvement with UMVIM began in the late seventies. At a gathering of the SEJ mission secretaries, I heard Tom Curtis share enthusiastically the vision God had given him about this vital mission ministry. At that time I was struck by the fact that the Atlanta UMVIM office was already in a financial struggle for its life, and I came back to get my own conference on board with support.
>
> Serving on the UMVIM board and participating in the rallies at Lake Junaluska have enriched my life immeasurably. However, the most wonderful privilege that UMVIM has afforded me has been that of forming eternal relationships of love in the bonds of Christ's love.

This conference has been one of the strongest in financial support of the UMVIM-SEJ office since it was first organized. At that time each district was asked to give fifty dollars annually, but Alabama/West Florida soon increased its giving to three hundred dollars per district per year. They also have in effect a policy that requires all recognized conference teams to register with the UMVIM office and subscribe to its insurance plan.

In 1997, a conference-wide effort was made by Bishop William Morris, conference UMVIM leaders, and several district superintendents to provide proper housing for pastors in the Demopolis District. The Reverend Charlie Williams, pastor, and his wife, Ella, expressed their joy and appreciation at the service of dedication conducted by Bishop Morris, who called the event "a marvelous day in the district and conference."

Florida Conference

The Reverend H. W. Parker, pastor of Christ Community Church in Jacksonville and a pioneer of this movement, wrote of the early years:

> In 1967 while serving another church in Florida, I realized that sermons, songs, and suppers were never going to change the local church, and certainly not change the world. A question that had been within me for several years was answered. Contemplating what a local church could do to change its ministry and mission, I felt the Lord suggesting, "Why not take three or four of your laypeople and visit some mission field and see firsthand what the needs are. Come home and share your discoveries with the local church, and let's see what will happen."

Just over two years later in March 1970 the Lord shared this same concept with Marlow Baxter, a member of St. John's United Methodist Church in Winter Haven where Parker was then serving. H. W. recalled:

> After sharing with me what the Lord had shared with him, Baxter and I both knew the time had come for sending laypeople from a local church to a mission area and finding projects for service. After a year of preparation and encouragement from Dr. Harry Haines, chief executive for UMCOR, we began with a journey to the Bahamas and then to Belize, Central America. This was the beginning of our "search-and-relate" teams, sent to check out and survey prospective mission projects.

Parker and the Reverend Delmas Copeland represented the Florida Conference at a consultation in Atlanta in 1974 called by the Reverend Bill Starnes, then SEJ field representative for the General Board of Missions. Representatives came from several annual conferences in the Southeast to consider this concept of personalizing mission by a hands-on experience. At that gathering Starnes is reported to have said, "St. John's Church is the catalyst in our calling this meeting. When the history of United Methodist missions is completed, this day will be marked as one of the most historic days ever." Bill went on to declare that "volunteer missions will be the wave of the future." Today Bill says, "I rejoice that this has already come to pass." The St. John's Church mission emphasis known as An Effort for Others eventually became Short-Term Volunteers, and finally United Methodist Volunteers In Mission. H. W. Parker recalled with much delight, "the unique revelation first to me in 1968 and then to Marlow Baxter in 1970, of how lay people were sent to do missions, and how the local church felt that they were the senders of their own people."

Out of this congregation came Charles and Jo Ann Selph, a lay couple who dedicated themselves for a period of service in Haiti beginning in August 1976 as the first coordinators for volunteers going to that island country. Both have endeared themselves to countless Haitians and volunteers for their loving and caring support over the years. Another significant outcome was the impact of this mission ministry on the St. John's Church itself. Budget deficits were overcome. Conference financial commitments were met ahead of time. Church membership grew. And a new sanctuary was built to accommodate two Sunday services, all credited to this new and powerful commitment to mission. Many other churches could report similar experiences as a result of their involvement in this movement.

In the late 1970s the Florida Conference organized its own conference UMVIM Committee, which has grown in strength over the years. Its purpose is to help equip local churches, districts, and individuals who want to serve with guidance as to projects and proper orientation. Most districts now have an UMVIM representative whose task is to keep anyone in the district fully informed of possible openings for volunteer service. The committee sponsors an annual rally each September. A presentation of the "Golden Hammer Award" is made each year to an outstanding Volunteer In Mission.

Florida has been heavily engaged not only in sending teams and individual volunteers but also in receiving them. More than eight thousand United Methodist volunteers came to the Dade County and Miami area after Hurricane Andrew to assist in that massive relief effort. In addition, many volunteers are constantly working with the large and growing refugee groups from Cuba, Haiti, and other places.

Holston Conference

One of the earliest pioneer leaders in the UMVIM movement, the Reverend John Trundle, was from this conference. I asked John about the rationale for the petition that he drafted for the SEJ Steering Committee to the 1980 General Conference dealing with the movement. He wrote, "The reason some of us wanted to make that petition to affirm the UMVIM concept was that we wanted to cooperate and coordinate our work teams and other activities through the General Board of Global Ministries. We wanted their cooperation and assistance. We also wanted to be a legitimate child of United Methodism and to work through regular church channels. We did not want to be independent. But we did not want or need to be controlled by the big bureaucracy."

Much of the work in the Holston Conference, which began around 1964, has been done directly by individual churches and people. One of the early leaders was the Reverend Ed Eldridge, who was sent to the Caribbean to look for places of need in addition to Haiti, which was receiving many teams from Holston. In 1979, Ed became consumed with assisting the Methodist Church on the island of Dominica, ravaged by Hurricane David. The government had given an abandoned military camp to the church. All but the gymnasium was open to the skies, and Holston was invited to help in the massive renovation. Ed took the first team in January 1980 to start the science building, eventually completing the project seven years and twenty-two teams later. In addition, a dental clinic and a house for the principal were constructed. Several students were sponsored for further education in this country to train for service back at St. Andrew's Methodist High School. Each year an optometrist, Dr. Bill Sullins and his wife, Martha, participated. Once he treated an elderly man and put a pair of glasses on him. Turning his patient around, Dr. Sullins asked, "Can you see the door?" The excited man said, "I can see the door *knob!*"

One significant development in the Holston Conference has been the work of the United Methodist Women through the UMVIM office. One of their leaders, Charlene Asbury, took a conference team of UMW members to Liberia in 1989 and started construction of a prenatal clinic at Ganta Hospital. Nancy Headlee of Loudon worked at the mission's leprosy center. Expecting to see crippled, deformed, almost lifeless children there, she found eight or nine who tagged along as she performed her duties, doing a kick dance while everyone held hands. "They are just like children at home. We are all one," said Headlee. Another team member, Julia Cushman, found determination in battling despair. She said, "Everything we see is made-to-order for discouragement. Our hosts in Liberia were Bill and Grace Warnock, missionaries from Holston, whose spirit is incredible. Their attitude is what I will take home with me."

The Holston UMW's first UMVIM trip was actually in 1987 to both Dominica and St. Maarten. Then came the Liberia visit, followed in 1991 by a trip to the Ana Gonzada Children's Home in Rio de Janeiro, a trip to the Rio Grande Conference in 1993, and a trip to Nicaragua in 1995.

Bishop Ray W. Chamberlain of the Holston Area has long been a friend and supporter of UMVIM. This was obvious when I first knew him as a pastor in the Virginia Conference. While president of the SEJ Fellowship of Conference Mission Secretaries, he went with a group of us to New York to put our case before Global Ministries, and he did so most persuasively. Chamberlain claimed that "boards and agencies tend to think 'programming' rather than 'movement'—to organize and institutionalize rather than get out of the way so the Spirit can flow through. Our task as missionary secretaries was to encourage GBGM to get out of the way, for as I said then, this is bigger than a plan or a program—it is God moving in a new way."

Kentucky Conference

During the last ten years the former Kentucky Conference (before merger with the Louisville Conference in 1996) sent about sixty-six teams to other countries, fourteen to other states, and thirty within the conference, with a total of about 1,660 volunteers. In twenty years of participation in the movement, Kentucky sent ninety-nine teams on international projects, nineteen to other states and thirty-eight for work at home, with a total of more than 2,100 volunteers.

A tragic event happened on April 3, 1974, when a tornado destroyed two-thirds of the town of Brandenburg, Kentucky, in the former Louisville Conference. Every house in the community was destroyed. A check from UMCOR arrived to assist the recovery operation, and volunteers poured in from across the country. Soon afterwards Harry Haines of UMCOR spoke at a mission rally and challenged the conference to assist in building a much-needed school building in Burrell Boom, Belize. As the conference had been the recipient of volunteer ministries, the challenge now was to respond to help others. The challenge became a clarion call. More than $40,000 was raised and forty-six volunteers were recruited.

Ben Thomson, first chair of the Louisville Conference UMVIM Committee, answered a call to restore a lay training center at the historical site of the Methodist Church District Office in Kingston, Jamaica. Four teams were dispatched to Kingston in 1978 and $20,000 was raised toward construction materials.

Another leader in the development of this ministry in the old Louisville Conference was Bobby Morrison, a businessman from Columbia. He said his interest started when he read about plans of the conference to send a team of volunteers to Belize. He went with the team and, upon return, planned for a reunion of team members, which became an annual practice that has lasted for many years. In 1976 Bobby decided to take his whole family on a team to Haiti, which further encouraged his participation.

By 1979 the Louisville Conference was asked to consider tackling some truly rugged terrain, the mountains in Haiti on the impoverished island of La Gonave just off the Haitian coast. This they did with zeal. According to Morrison, "We worked on projects in

Belize, Haiti, Jamaica, Dominican Republic, Honduras, Mexico. We also worked on many local projects, in disaster relief after Hurricane Andrew and floods in Mississippi, and a youth mission team to Mexico. UMVIM gave us an education that money cannot buy. I have seen dramatic change in the lives of a multitude of people. Their priorities have changed. They're taking a more active part, and several have gone into full-time mission or other church ministries. As I reflect on it, I believe UMVIM has been the most profound influence on my life."

The Louisville Conference, like some others, has an outstanding record of tackling a major construction project, sending several teams with funds to assist in an undertaking that demands strong support and involvement. One such case was on behalf of a new Methodist Church in Costa Rica some years ago. When the building was ready for dedication, the bishop in San Jose invited Louisville's Bishop Paul Duffey to come and preach, which he did. This was an occasion of much rejoicing on the part of Costa Rican Methodists and representatives of the teams. It also helped a stateside bishop better understand our ministry as volunteers.

One of the key leaders in the Louisville Conference development was Patricia Wagner, ably assisted by her husband, Jerry. Patricia says, "The UMVIM movement in our conference, as in many others, was the most vital movement of the United Methodist Church during the 1970s and 1980s. The church profited greatly from the revitalization of members who became involved in helping themselves by helping others. I discovered my own leadership potential through serving as a conference UMVIM officer. Helping our conference become more involved locally as well as internationally was most rewarding."

Later Pat served as a staff member of the Volunteers In Mission office of the General Board of Global Ministries. Then she and Jerry served for three years as coordinators for volunteers going to Jamaica.

The Kentucky Conference has had a strong medical component to its work. Judy Neal, a nurse from Lexington, has for the past eleven years been a part of medical mission teams to Costa Rica, Belize, St. Vincent, Zaire, and Uganda. "As a teenager, I dreamed of one day being a missionary. But then came marriage and children, and that dream got put on hold. Later I shared my dream with a minister friend who told me about UMVIM and got me on my first team. That was the beginning, and God has used UMVIM to help me grow spiritually and personally more than I could have imagined. Five years ago I could not have been persuaded to say more than a sentence prayer in public. But now I speak to many medical groups, Sunday school classes, and others."

Judy often has accompanied Dr. James and Linda Fields on the medical programs to St. Vincent in the south Caribbean. She shares another story of young Andre of St. Vincent, who was brought to the team by his mother. At five years of age, this young lad had never spoken a word, being severely tongue-tied. "We laid him down on a school table, anesthetized his mouth, and clipped under his tongue. When we were done, we asked him to stick out his tongue. He could only get it to the tip of his teeth. We laid him back down and clipped some more. This time when we asked him to stick out his tongue, he could almost touch his nose. He said 'Mama' for the very first time!"

In 1994 Judy was a member of a Global Ministries team that went to Goma in Zaire to work with Rwandan refugees. She reported that the horrors of war, especially on children, defy description. She told of a child whose parents were both killed right in front of her. Judy shared her frustrations with a volunteer doctor, who reminded her that her presence alone was a means of comfort and strength to others. Judy's stories from her mission trips to several countries could fill a book.

Memphis Conference

A faithful leader in the Memphis Conference is Dr. Solomon Christian, a dentist and vice-president of the UMVIM Medical Fellowship. Dr. Christian has participated as a medical member of several teams, and has led an investigating team from the SEJ to India, to conduct negotiations with their bishops about future work in his home country. He reported, "Three formal meetings were held among the team, Indian bishops, and other leaders of the Methodist Church in India. The Reverend John Martin, then president of the UMVIM-SEJ board, and Dr. Christian explained how UMVIM seeks to work in cooperation with and under the direction of our hosts in other lands. A new bond was formed, which bodes well for the future of our mission together."

A friend of Dr. Christian, the Reverend Samson Parekh of the Methodist Bible Seminary in Gujarat, India, was quite impressed by these visitors. He wrote:

It was eye-popping to see the work team perform these manual tasks under the unbearably hot sun. Their intense labor revealed to me their commitment to the Lord and passion for the people and the Methodist Church in India. I am convinced that only the divine inspiration and provision can bring this kind of unique ministry into existence and can make it function continually to meet the needs of needy people in a most unusual and significant way.

Dr. Christian has developed a program he calls Families In Mission. He commented, "It has been said that families who pray together, stay together. But for many parents the challenge becomes one of how to translate the family's prayerful relationship with Christ into a living, breathing, tangible expression of Christ's love for us and our love for others. This is the purpose of Families In Mission."

The Christians' daughter, Monica, wrote about her involvement with UMVIM as a high-school sophomore:

Ever since I was in the second grade, my family and I have been going to the UMVIM rally and Medical Fellowship meeting at Lake Junaluska. I had always thought you had to be an adult in order to participate on a team. My father proved me wrong when he led a Families In Mission team to the Reelfoot Rural Ministry in Tennessee, and I was a team member. Our group worked on a house badly in need of repairs. We finished painting it and put in much-needed shelves. A few of us had to go back on a return trip to actually complete the job. I am glad I chose to start doing UMVIM work in my teenage years because it is definitely a disease I can never be cured of. Now the disease will spread and spread until my body can't contain it. When that happens, I hope the contagion will spread to others so they too will see how it feels to help someone in need.

This conference, under the leadership of Joseph Geary, has had a special interest in the country of Estonia. As a leader of one of the teams to Estonia, Nancy Eubanks describes a moving scene:

Americans were handing out leaflets advertising a coming Bible school at Agape United Methodist Church in the city of Parnu. Dr. Barry Scott was making balloon sculptures and giving them to children. He had made hearts, monkeys, dogs, cats, crazy hats; and the children were all pushing and grabbing for one of their own. I looked closely and saw that Barry had made a cross, a blue balloon cross, and was holding it in the air, and they were reaching for it—all those little grimy, scarred, bruised, empty hands trying to get this symbol of hope and love and beauty in their lives.

Mississippi Conference

"My first knowledge of UMVIM came as an announcement from my pastor, the Reverend Bill Lott, one Sunday morning in June 1976," says W. P. Cox, an active member of the North Mississippi Conference and author of a ten-year history of conference UMVIM ministry. "He told us that the South Carolina Conference was sending a group to build a parsonage in Haiti, and he thought Millsaps Dye and I should go along and help on the project. Ruth Stoddard said, 'Cox, if you go, you will never be the same when you return.' And she was right!"

Their next mission was also to Haiti. Cox reports:

This was an entirely different world to all fifteen members of our team. We learned to share. We learned to accept Christian people as our sisters and brothers. These people, though extremely poor, had not lost their pride. A local man said to me, "We are poor, but don't laugh at us." On a trip to Belize, I remember a worker who was making $5 a month had been given a hand saw by a team member from Virginia. When he received his monthly pay, he gave $1 back to the superintendent, who asked what it was for. The worker told him "I want to pay for the hand saw." I always like to emphasize that mission is a two-way street. We are all givers and all receivers.

Mexico was a land that seemed to beckon to us next. Tom Curtis organized a visitation mission in 1980 with representatives from a number of SEJ annual conferences. All of us accepted projects, which in a sense opened wide a new door of service through which many have gone. For us from North Mississippi, the big undertaking was at Salamanca, where I later helped dedicate a new social hall and sanctuary we had worked on. Bishop Ulises Hernandez was an active part of that team, having laid the foundation stone for the new church. Another major project was in Panama, where Danny Rowland coordinated a flow of teams providing much assistance in renovating the huge church and school in the city of David.

In the former Mississippi Conference, one of the main leaders was Earl Greenough. Earl took an early interest in a huge project in Jamaica—the renovation of the Grateful Hill Church, severely damaged by an earthquake years ago. He led a number of teams, raised funds and saw that this important historic place was properly restored as a center of worship.

Bishop Meadors wrote, "In Mississippi, my goal has been to provide an opportunity for every person I ordain to participate in an UMVIM experience. I am seeking to work in partnership with UMVIM as we respond to the needs of God's most vulnerable children. As long as the church is involved in God's mission in the world, there is a future and a hope."

North Alabama Conference

The Reverend Ray Crump led a team to Chile in 1975, sparking a renewed interest in mission in North Alabama, and was the motivating force behind the formation of an UMVIM task force in 1977. When Lawton Higgs became conference chair in 1982, he gave special emphasis to establishing UMVIM district task forces. His successor, Robert Sparkman, brought renewed enthusiasm, which resulted in a major increase in the number of participants.

Conference chairs Donald and Lulu Stewart convinced Global Ministries of the need for UMVIM teams to Panama to help replace a housing project destroyed by the US invasion. This was the first time the World Division officially asked UMVIM to take on a specific project. The Stewarts are also giving important leadership to a new UMVIM-SEJ program of evangelism among the poor.

Students from Birmingham-Southern College have been regular participants in this ministry over a number of years. Led by the Reverend Stewart Jackson, campus minister, they have concentrated their efforts in Zimbabwe as a means of understanding international affairs in the life of the church. One of their number, Ben Roberts, went as a medical student for an extended period of service in a Kenyan Methodist Hospital in order to broaden his awareness of opportunities for medical service later.

North Carolina Conference

Work teams were first recognized in 1973 in this conference through the leadership of the Reverend Ernest Porter, director of outreach. A sixteen-person team from the conference was sent to Chapare, Bolivia, on a medical, construction, and evangelistic mission. From that first experience, a partnership in mission was formed that has grown rapidly in strength and has become a powerful instrument for church renewal, mission interpretation, changing priorities, and lifestyles to meet the needs of the world.

The following year a team was sent from the Edenton Street UMC in Raleigh to work in San Pedro, Bolivia. Several more teams went the next year, and the work has continued to grow year by year. One of the major emphases of the North Carolina Conference has been on adequate preparation and training for mission. Its orientation program is a helpful model for other conferences to consider.

In 1986 the conference celebrated its tenth year as an organized UMVIM group. From a small beginning in 1973 the work has increased remarkably. Mary Whanger, former missionary to Zimbabwe and chair of the conference UMVIM committee from 1980 to 1988, credits much of the early and enthusiastic start to Julia McLean Williams, a former missionary to Bolivia. She wrote, "Julia, more than any other person, was responsible for the early growth of UMVIM in this conference." Two team members from these early years, Mike and Hope Ward, kept careful records of all team activity, which provided material from which came the first *UMVIM-SEJ Handbook*. Teams have gone to Barbados, Bolivia, Chile, Costa Rica, Haiti, Jamaica, Mexico, Peru, and the South Caribbean. Closer to home, teams have served in the Hardee Mission in Florida, John's Island in South Carolina, Henderson Settlement in Kentucky, and the Appalachia Service Project in Tennessee, as well as in a number of in-conference church building programs.

In 1990 the conference Construction Program was started through the conference Board of Mission with the support of a Duke Endowment. The program's purpose has been to assist struggling congregations with much-needed facilities, whether sanctuary, parsonage, or social hall. Gary Smith, construction coordinator for conference projects, reported that:

> the demand for major construction projects has been so great that we have concentrated on these projects and referred smaller ones to UMVIM and individual churches. While it takes longer for us to do so with volunteers, we generally complete projects at a half to two-thirds of the bid price. In 1995 we added a full-time assistant, which allows us to keep a work team supervised and frees me to devote the necessary time to planning, sourcing materials, and dealing with subcontractors.
>
> One of my favorite experiences involves a team member from our first project. She was an architect who had taken retirement. Someone finally talked her into joining a team to help on our building project. This gave her a new direction, and since then she has been on a number of other teams.

Mary Whanger also served as secretary for the UMVIM-SEJ Steering Committee (predecessor to our Board of Directors) for the same period, three of those years as dean of the UMVIM-SEJ rally. She wrote, "We who go to minister often find ourselves being ministered to at our deepest levels. It is a humbling, freeing, enriching experience, and those to whom this is given are permanently changed."

The next chair was Annette Bingham, whose husband, Bill, grew up in Jamaica and felt a special concern for that island country. This culminated in their conference taking on a large project, known as Operation Peace, requiring about a dozen teams in the city of Kingston. This building was constructed in a part of the community known for its violence and next door to the historic Wesley Methodist Church. Upon completion, Raleigh Area Bishop C. P. Minnick participated in the service of dedication which drew a massive crowd, including the Governor General of Jamaica.

A number of individuals from the conference have provided valuable service as volunteers for extended periods of time. One such example is Nancie Allen, who spent a year-and-a-half at the Red Bird Mission school as an assistant to the music director, which gave her great opportunities to share with the children in their singing and in their dramas at school performances.

William "Bill" Gross of Sanford is an information technology professional, active in leading teams. At the rally in 1984 Dr. Watson, as UMVIM chair, made an appeal for someone with computer skills to develop a program to manage UMVIM's phenomenal growth and complexity. Bill responded enthusiastically and came to Atlanta regularly to establish NOAH, Network of Opportunities Abroad and at Home, thus launching UMVIM technology to meet the twenty-first century. Bill has been available as a consultant on a regular basis ever since. In addition, he has edited and designed publications and still manages to take many teams on work projects. Back in North Carolina, he and his wife, Melissa, work on the publication staff of their conference UMVIM newsletter.

North Georgia Conference

One of the first chairs in this conference was Dr. Quillian Hamby, a dentist who was a member of Grace Church in Atlanta. Dr. Hamby provided fine leadership at the early stages of development. He was followed by Dr. Bill Hinson, a former missionary to Brazil. Bill led a number of teams himself and arranged for an annual rally in which volunteers could enjoy fellowship, meet members from other teams, and plan for future work.

One near disaster occurred when Bill was leading a team to a small island off the coast of Honduras. The plane lost power as it was returning to the mainland, but managed to belly-land on a pineapple field which cushioned it sufficiently so that no one was injured. Another team Hinson led worked in Jamaica at St. Ann's

Bay in the early stages of the new Wesley High School. Two members of the group were Jessie and Lewistine McCoy, retired missionaries to Latin America and former staff in the Latin American office of the General Board of Global Ministries. Jessie wrote, "It was a lot of fun, and we're glad we were part of the group."

One year a record number of twenty-nine teams from North Georgia were handled through the SEJ office directly, as the conference committee was not functioning. This did not include teams of North Georgia United Methodist Men, who have worked separately.

Perhaps the first team from this conference was led by the Reverend William Holt to Bolivia, where he had formerly served as a missionary in 1967. Together with other doctors from North Carolina and South Carolina, this North Georgia team, primarily out of Carrollton, treated Indians in remote villages where no doctors were available. Since then, Dr. Holt has been a part of many other teams, including a 1994 medical team back to Bolivia. Other active team leaders have been William Scott of LaGrange, Marie Bond of Royston, Dr. John E. Stansell of Winder, and John Van Horn of Smyrna. Athens First Church has had a long history of UMVIM service, particularly to Costa Rica.

In 1994 I received an urgent call from Dr. John Wesley Z. Kurewa, vice-chancellor of Africa University in Zimbabwe. He was calling, he said, to issue an SOS, an emergency appeal for us to send teams to help in constructing about a dozen new staff houses desperately needed on campus. He remembered well that only two years previously we had responded to his first appeal to send teams to help renovate abandoned farm buildings so they could serve as the initial campus. I recalled that one Atlanta pastor, the Reverend Robert Winstead, told me, "Any time you have an emergency call for a team, let me know. I will be glad to try to organize and be ready." So I called Bob and within a short time his group was off to Zimbabwe as the first team to start the staff-housing project.

North Georgia teams have served in many areas including Hinton Rural Life Center, Lake Junaluska Assembly, repairs to existing church buildings in the conference, and hurricane, tornado, and flood disaster relief. Other countries served include Panama, Costa Rica, Jamaica, Haiti, Honduras, Brazil, Kenya, and Indonesia.

The year 1993 was especially significant in that it witnessed the sending forth of the first all-African-American UMVIM team through the SEJ office. This group came from the Bethel and Ben Hill United Methodist Churches in Atlanta, with Sandra Lacefield as team leader. Encouraged by the UMVIM director, the group accepted the suggestion of serving in Zimbabwe. Their project would be to paint one of the dormitories at Nyamuzuwe High School, located in a remote rural area. On the way out from Harare, the bus carrying the group of fourteen broke down, and they were stranded from eight o'clock at night until nearly midnight. About that time the local district superintendent, the Reverend Sandy Sanganzah, came looking for the UMVIM team, passing right by them at first! He was expecting to find a mostly white group, certainly not one composed entirely of African Americans.

Lacefield and her team returned home enthusiastic about their mission and about their support of Africa University. They have since taken teams to Jamaica and South Africa. Sandra was elected to the UMVIM-SEJ board. She now serves as secretary and has been dean of the annual UMVIM rally.

A number of exceptional individuals have gone forth from this conference as volunteers. They include Stacey Delarber of Peachtree Road United Methodist Church who served ten months in Australia as assistant director of the Somerville Family and Children Community Services, a program of the Uniting Church in Australia in the Darwin area. Another volunteer from that same church was Robin Harp, who served in the former East Germany in a difficult situation dealing with refugees. The UMW conference president arranged for her supervision and accommodation with much interest. Robin was instrumental in bringing forth a measure of reconciliation among some of the divided sections of the community.

Another North Georgia person who served as an individual volunteer is W. Curt LaFrance, Jr., of Mt. Pisgah Church in Atlanta. Curt intended to become a medical doctor and was anxious for some exposure to medical practice, more than he could get in this country. Arrangements were worked out for him by the office to serve at the Maua Methodist Hospital in Kenya. He wrote:

Culturally, I found it necessary to leave behind the biases and prejudices ingrained in me from my youth so that I would see African people not only as equals but as ones whom I would serve in the name of Christ. Politically, I came to understand that through Christ's witness, the church should reconcile conflict and manifest the love and peace in her life by being an example to all nations. The time in Maua through UMVIM has forever affected my life. There the Lord prepared my heart for a lifetime of service to him through medicine in the name of Christ.

Red Bird Missionary Conference

This area in Central and Eastern Kentucky is located in the heart of Appalachia and has been on the hosting end for many teams across the whole country. According to the Reverend David L. Allen, former Kentucky Conference Mission secretary, "From the early days of Henderson Settlement and Red Bird Mission, work teams have built, repaired, painted, and gone about innumerable tasks that have greatly advanced the outreach of both of these centers of our church."

"But volunteers from within the Red Bird Missionary Conference have also responded to the need of others outside southeastern Kentucky," Allen pointed out. They have sought to return good for good to others in a remarkable manner. The spirit of Red Bird itself is none other than the spirit of volunteerism.

South Carolina Conference

One of the original sponsoring conferences in UMVIM in the Southeast, South Carolina remains one of the key leaders in its development. The name of Dr. Michael C. Watson is synonymous with the Volunteers In Mission movement almost everywhere, and certainly in his home state. The conference presented a plaque to him in April 1997 on his retirement as conference chair after thirty years of devoted service.

The country that has received most attention from South Carolina is Haiti. A remarkable ophthalmic program begun in 1974 by Dr. Hal Crosswell has continued over the years. Eye-care physicians from across the USA work in two-week rotations for three months each spring in one of the most remote parts of the island to provide the finest modern eye care on the entire island to isolated villagers.

South Carolina has been in Haiti for an agricultural program coordinated by Joe Cal Watson, Mike's brother. To help one village seriously in need of an access road, Joe asked Grace Church in North Augusta to contribute $1,000 dollars to buy hand tools, sledge hammers, axes, picks, and shovels to build a four-foot-wide path through the bush. The path was built and the tools passed on to other villagers. Development work continues on a larger scale by two technically trained community-development workers employed by the church through Joe Cal's generosity. Joe has spoken to literally hundreds of churches, has never turned down a request to speak, and has given the opportunity for thousands of people to participate, not vicariously but in a more personal way, in the mission of the church. Often he is asked to come back to give a progress report on how the program is doing.

In a short article, "Why I Have Continued to Go to Haiti for a Quarter of a Century," Joe Watson has many tales to share. He wrote:

> To arrive in Port-au-Prince in 1970 was like living an adventure movie. I searched each face for John Wayne or Humphrey Bogart. It was with a missionary family, the Ormond McConnells, that I was first introduced to some of the Haitian foods of which I have become so fond. Later it was in Jeremie, where my main work was to center in the beginning, that I was introduced to the Haitian people who have proved to be some of the most delightful, warmhearted, loving people I have ever seen, and consider myself blessed to have associated with them. In five days I established friendships that are still maintained and revered today.
>
> My return back to Port-au-Prince was not by air but by boat which was overloaded with people and animals. We moved out of the bay, only to be met by one of the worst storms you can imagine, but finally managed to escape the wind. I was on the boat some twenty-six hours with 300 to 500 persons. There was no water, food, life preserver, fire

extinguisher, or sign of a sanitary facility. But it is my firm belief that this trip was the beginning of my love affair with the Haitian people. The care and concern shown me, a complete stranger of a different race from a foreign country, by the other passengers in my cabin, is something that will never be forgotten, and the memories of this trip will be cherished forever. And let me add, I was a day late for jury duty, but the judge said I had the best excuse he had ever heard.

Another of the pioneer leaders in UMVIM-SEJ was the Reverend Needham Williamson of South Carolina. He became a member of his conference committee in 1970 and led the first overseas team helping to build a forty-by-seventy-foot medical clinic in Jeremie, Haiti.

By 1974, various names for this group that became UMVIM were being used, such as the work-team committee, short-term volunteers, and short-term volunteers in mission. In July of that year, Williamson proposed, and it was agreed by the South Carolina Conference, that the name "Volunteers In Mission" become the official designation of the movement. Two years later when I came on board, it seemed wise to add the name of our denomination, so UMVIM became our official name. This would be similar to the Presbyterian Volunteers In Mission program, after which I modeled our early work. This was in keeping with the acronym used by the United Methodist Committee on Relief (UMCOR) and seemed to make good sense to our leaders.

Williamson remembers attending the first organizational meeting in 1974, called by Bill Starnes to address the idea of developing some appropriate response to this growing movement. He wrote about:

> one representative from the General Board of Global Ministries who discouraged our moving in this direction of developing an organization to meet our needs. He wanted any such efforts to be under the supervision of the General Board. I distinctly remember one layman saying to him in the presence of more than 100 persons, "We want this movement to be under the umbrella of the United Methodist Church [meaning in cooperation with the General Board], but rest assured it will move forward with or without your support." And was that ever a prophetic statement!

In the January 1996 issue of the *South Carolina United Methodist Advocate,* an article "UMVIM: A Hard Story to Tell, But Once Told, This Story Changes Lives," the Reverend C. E. Kanipe told of seeking advice on telling the story of volunteer missions from the Reverend George Strait, one of the earliest pioneers in the movement going back some twenty-seven years. George said, "It will probably be one of the hardest things you've ever tried to do. It will be hard to know where to begin. There are so many projects, so many stories. Everyone comes back with his or her own story. In those early days, no one could have predicted the phenomenal growth that the Volunteers In Mission movement would see. It was simply a matter of responding to human need by tapping into the resources and goodwill of United Methodist people. The movement that developed was of the Holy Spirit, not of human design." To which we can all say amen.

South Georgia Conference

The Conference Youth Council in 1975 made plans to send teams of about five teenagers and one adult to work on mission projects across South Georgia. The youth often led vacation church school and other youth activities after the physical work of repairs during the daytime hours.

The Conference UMVIM Committee was organized in 1978. Some of the early projects were to John's Island, South Carolina, and to the Open Door Community Center in Columbus. Then teams ventured out to Haiti, Costa Rica, and Mexico. During that summer the first of many teams was sent to the Choctaw Indian Reservation in Philadelphia, Mississippi, a practice that has continued as one of the conference's major mission outreach projects with excellent results. Later teams have been sent to Trinidad, St. Maarten, Anguilla, Jamaica, Liberia, Costa Rica, and to an agricultural project in Haiti developed by Wesley Kaylor.

Doris Songer of St. Luke Church in Columbus wrote of her experiences in Haiti:

The overwhelming impression of Haiti was one of so many people and so much poverty. The people are very resourceful, making use of everything. I

saw luggage made from soft-drink cans, a small oil lamp made from a con-
densed milk can; and the children use goat vertebrae for jacks. All the food
scraps are used to feed animals. Nothing is thrown away. A question arose
as to whether it was wise to spend money on the trip rather than sending
money for Haitians to use. Missionary Betty Darby responded, saying she had
the same question several years before. However, she sees much good from
the work teams. The Haitian people know of the conveniences in other countries. The fact that people are willing to give up these things and come to live
and work side by side with them makes a deep impression on them about
God's love for all people.

Another major project for this conference was to assist in building a new Lake Independence Church, later to be named St. Luke
Church, in Belize. This project, consisting of about a dozen teams,
was coordinated by Jeanie Blankenbaker. After several years of
hard work, the church was completed and ready for dedication on
December 30, 1990. Team member Mamie Moore of St. Luke
Church in Columbus was there. She reported, "Going to Belize for
the dedication were sixteen members of the South Georgia
Conference, which included Bishop Richard Looney. His presence
added to the significance of the occasion."

The Pittman Park Church in Statesboro has had an unusual
amount of involvement in this ministry. When the Reverend Larry
Roberts was pastor, he invited a missionary doctor serving in
Ecuador to share his experiences of work with the Quechua
Indians. This visit inspired the church to send its own teams, first
to Belize and later to many other lands as well as to projects in this
country. International projects have been served in Ecuador,
Panama, Brazil, Belize, Venezuela, Cuba, Zimbabwe, Jamaica,
Anguilla, and St. Maarten.

One of the most faithful and regular team leaders has been Dr.
George Evans of Dublin. He has led medical teams for over a dozen
years to the St. Ann's Hospital in Jamaica. George has so endeared
himself to the local people in the community that they have named
a wing of the hospital after him. In addition to his medical work,
he has also participated in renovating a nearby clinic that was in
bad shape. Dr. Evans has been kind enough to allow young med-

ical students to be members of his teams, especially in the summer months.

Perhaps the longest-serving officer of the South Georgia UMVIM Committee has been the Reverend Jack McCullough, who was responsible for starting an annual rally and training event each October in South Georgia. After retirement the Reverend George Herndon and his wife, Cora, have been active, particularly in Jamaica, with multi-faceted teams doing construction, evangelism, and Bible school. George has also concentrated on helping with a number of in-conference projects. A volunteer lay evangelist who served in Russia, Lucretia Maddox, reports that her ministry there was blessed of God.

The Gay's Hill Baptist Church in South Georgia was one of many black congregations to suffer loss due to arson. James and Hilda Dutrow have been responsible on behalf of the UMVIM-SEJ office for coordinating all volunteers coming to assist in this type of renovation project from across the country. This is another example of the leadership being offered by this movement to the entire United Methodist Church.

Tennessee Conference

UMVIM started in the Tennessee Conference in 1978 with its first team to Dangriga, Belize, led by the Reverend Ed Blackburn and the Reverend Tom Cloyd. Ed had joined a team from the Louisville Conference to Belize the previous year in order to learn about leading a team. Norris Allen, who went on to become the principal leader in the conference for many years, wrote, "I was a member of that first team from Tennessee and have been working with teams ever since. Being a contractor by trade for nearly thirty years, I feel God has blessed my life with rich memories of each trip. My work has included Belize, Jamaica, St. Vincent, Dominica, Grenada including Carricou, Puerto Rico, St. Maarten, and Honduras. I have also been on teams that repaired hurricane damage in Alabama and Florida as well as many projects in Tennessee."

One day at the office I received a call from Norris telling me something had happened that he had always feared. One member of his team, Ed Vaughn, had died of a heart attack. Norris

informed the Methodist pastor and the nearest USA official immediately. The body was returned home, and I was able to be present
for a very moving memorial service. Vaughn's widow asked that a
memorial fund be established at his Gideon United Methodist
Church in Greenbrier.

For the last several years, Norris and many others from the
Tennessee Conference have gone to LaCeiba on the Honduran
coast to share in the ministry of the Reverend Phillip and Sandra
Beisswenger who served for four years at LaCeiba. Their appointment marked the first time UMVIM had placed a couple for regular full-time missionary service.

The next chair of the Tennessee Conference committee was Glenn
Abernathy, an engineer who took on large responsibility in Panama
in preparation for teams to come and help with a major house
building program. This was to be a follow-up to the loss of homes
damaged or destroyed in the USA invasion shortly before. Glenn
constantly had to battle with local authorities about having a proper foundation for the dozens of houses to be built by future teams
from across the country. Some teams went, against our advice,
before the foundations were ready, to their great frustration.

Belmont United Methodist Church in Nashville is quite active in this
ministry, having given strong support to construction and medical
teams to St. Vincent. More recently the church has assisted with teams
to Mexico to finish construction of a small church, the name of which
in English means "God's Camp." According to Jodi Smith of Belmont,
"Several members from the Mexican church responded positively to an
invitation to visit our church. They worked on a variety of community
service projects for the Second Harvest Food Bank and the Community
Care Fellowship for homeless persons; helped refinish pews from the
old Caldwell Church; and got to experience Music City."

Bishop Kenneth Carder of the Nashville Area provides strong
support for UMVIM. While on an episcopal visit to Mexico in
January 1998 he was deeply touched by the ministry of Tennessee
volunteers. He explains:

In almost every community I visited, from the rural parishes in Mexico City to
the remote mountain village of Huitzapulah, I saw the work of United
Methodist volunteers from the United States. I visited one of the toughest

mission stations in the world, and the Tennessee Conference is there making a difference. Bethel Methodist Church, located in the Morelos neighborhood of Mexico City, is surrounded by poverty, crime, and human suffering. Across the street from the church are housing units built by the Methodist Church of Mexico following the terrible earthquake of 1986. Children play in the streets. Several elderly persons sit in front of the church where they find safety and friendliness. The church operates a little fruit and vegetable stand where people from the neighborhood can buy food at low cost.

The only playground in the neighborhood other than the street is a small area provided by the church. A health clinic is now available. The kitchen equipped by the Tennessee Conference volunteers provides food for the congregation and neighbors. A small apartment serves as transition housing for people who are in treatment for drug addiction. The living quarters for the pastor and his family have been upgraded by volunteers.

Inscribed on a concrete foundation are the words *Tennessee Conference*. The day before I visited, Beverly Beckwith, who coordinates our conference program, had been down preparing for the next team. The people spoke of her and the team members from Tennessee as friends and family. One person told me through an interpreter, "The people of Tennessee really care about us. They treat us with respect and love."

It is obvious that Volunteers In Mission do more than construct buildings, teach children, and provide medical care. They share themselves and in so doing, incarnate the Gospel. Volunteers are building more than concrete foundations for useful facilities. They are building relationships with other members of Christ's family and sharing in Christ's ministry of love.

Virginia Conference

The pioneer in this conference for Volunteers In Mission was Douglas True of Arlington. His special interest was the island of Haiti where he led many teams. Participation and interest suddenly skyrocketed in 1984 when it was decided to take on a conference-wide church building project, San Lucas Atoyatenco in Mexico. After this project was completed, twenty more teams eventually helped build a home for the aging in partnership with the Methodist women in Mexico's Central Conference.

During Dr. John Martin, Jr.'s, tenure as chair of the conference committee in the 1980s, an astounding 110 teams served, many going to Mexico and to emergency relief programs in this country. Dr. Martin reported that Virginia teams have participated in ethnic-minority local church projects. "We have received volunteers from within and outside our conference to assist in rebuilding a church and parsonage badly damaged by flood. We are experimenting with the United Methodist Men in constructing an infirmary and a district camp. We feel we have barely scratched the surface of volunteerism in our conference. Each year the participation has doubled from the year before." Stephen Rhodes succeeded Dr. Martin, and then was followed by Roy Creech who continued in this excellent tradition.

C. M. "Kip" Robinson of Richmond, present Conference chair, led a team from the Ashland District to Zimbabwe in 1993. Their work was to put a roof on the Mutowani UMC, a rural church in the northeastern part of the country. The church has been in existence about two decades, but could not be completed as there were no funds to complete the roof all at one time. A roof must be built all at one time in order to overcome the potential for warping, weathering, and attack by termites. The team worked hard with the local folk, completing twenty-one roof trusses and erecting them on top of the long-standing brick walls without the aid of any crane, except as they improvised. Kip said:

On the morning of the fifth day, disaster struck when all but four of the trusses fell down in light winds just after the team had left the inside of the building following devotions. The Africans took all of this in stride. The team members, however, were devastated. Was the entire trip destined to be a failure? We all worked together and the trusses were finally replaced. Two years later, while there on another project, we were invited back to the dedication of the Mutowani Church where the congregation had grown from about one hundred in 1993 to over five hundred on that Sunday.

Kip told about bearing a:

unique gift called a fairystone, which is found only in a small area of Virginia. Fairystones are in the shape of a cross. They were much prized by early Native

Americans in Virginia. Each stone was dedicated by the sponsoring Virginia church in anticipation of the dedication at Mutowani, taken 8,000 miles and given to the congregation at the dedication service. A precious stone to the indigenous people of America was given to the indigenous people of Zimbabwe. Were the connectional aspects of our great church clear? Only God will know for sure, but on a beautiful and glorious day in a rural Zimbabwe town, the connection of all people through the love of Christ was evident.

Betty Adams, an individual volunteer from Virginia, has participated in many projects across the world in the past ten years. She writes:

By profession, I am a school nurse. Because school nursing does not require me to use the latest complex technical equipment, I find it easier to work under conditions found in the Third World. I have served at Ganta Hospital in Liberia, worked in clinics in Jamaica, and helped with medical projects in Central America. In 1996 I experienced a Third World hospital from a different perspective when two of our mission team members were hit by a small truck in St. Ann's Bay, Jamaica. They were taken to the local government hospital. The injuries were not as serious as we had initially thought, but one member was required to stay overnight. I have never seen more love and compassion at any hospital. The medical treatment given there adhered to the same good principles we use in this country, even though their resources were limited.

Part of Betty's reason for going is "totally selfish. Sometimes I'm asked why I continue to go. After all, nothing changes. I should reply, 'I do. I change.' You see, I receive far more than I am able to give."

A special notation is made here to acknowledge the invaluable contribution made to this ministry by retired Bishop R. Kern Eutsler of Virginia who served us so well for seven years as director of promotion and interpretation. Bishop Eutsler established the Fellowship of One Thousand (FOOT), a program of enlisting one thousand churches and/or individuals to give one hundred dollars annually to the support of the UMVIM-SEJ office. He traveled far and wide across the Southeast, wrote innumerable letters, and made many calls to help us secure the necessary funding to keep the movement on a forward path.

Western North Carolina Conference

According to Joel and Faith Key, veterans of the UMVIM movement since its beginning days:

The conference building-team movement began when Dr. Horace McSwain, executive secretary of the Board of Missions, wrote to the Advance Department of the National Division and asked that arrangements be made for a group of laypersons to visit Methodist mission work in Puerto Rico. The trip was planned in 1963 with a group of ten persons who saw the destructive work of termites, buildings falling apart, no longer held erect by soggy ground. Team member Dr. N. M. "Nat" Harrison wanted to recruit laymen from the conference to go at their own expense to build a new chapel in Puerto Rico. This was done in 1964, but the flu epidemic put four of them in bed just days before departure.

Even before this, however, William Bobbitt had organized a team to Cuba in 1956, the first by the WNC Conference, according to his widow, Margaret B. Sills. She reports, "While in college and serving a student appointment, he hosted a Scandinavian Caravan for a week and that ignited the spark for his work in missions. It continued until his death. His outreach included Belize, Costa Rica, Bolivia, and several African countries. He has been credited as the moving spirit behind this conference's volunteer medical ministry."

The Reverend Donald Haynes led the team in 1965 to a project near the town of Arecibo in Puerto Rico. The biggest project thus far came in 1972 with the construction of Villa Fontana Church in Carolina, near San Juan. WNC Conference was further challenged by a request for three projects in Haiti in 1975. Until then, all money for materials for Puerto Rican projects had come from the National Division. Now it would be necessary to raise ten thousand dollars for the three projects in Haiti. Soon the conference was sending teams to Panama, Jamaica, Costa Rica, Aruba, Mexico, Nassau, South Africa, Guatemala, Brazil, Cuba, Alaska, Antigua, Barbados, and Kenya. A building team committee was formed to guide the rapidly developing program.

The next chair was Ed Cochran, followed by Tom Howard.

During Howard's leadership, the assignment of country coordinators was initiated. Experienced team leaders were appointed to coordinate the work in specific countries and the overall recruitment, arrangements, recommendation of projects in that country, and the selection of team members.

Louise Doyle was elected to serve as treasurer of the committee since it began in Dr. McSwain's office where she served as secretary. During her tenure, the first team was sent to South Africa and an emphasis was placed on student and youth teams. During 1997 thirty teams plus three youth teams were sent to nine countries. The committee provided about seventy thousand dollars in materials for the various projects.

A special feature of the WNC Conference is the fact that a number of years ago the Reverend Joe Ervin, who had been very active with work in Haiti, spoke to Bishop L. Scott Allen about his interest in helping with church construction in the conference. The bishop had chided him about his extensive mission interest away from home. Bishop Allen soon arranged for that appointment. Since then, Joe estimates, many hundreds of thousands of dollars have been saved by the use of volunteers in building and renovating church facilities across the conference.

This conference has the most centrally organized committee and program of any in this jurisdiction. Louise Doyle has served as treasurer since its inception. All work is planned by the committee. Any interested persons or groups must make their arrangements to join one of the teams being organized by the committee and follow their guidelines. The plans apparently work well for the United Methodists of Western North Carolina.

The General Board of Global Ministries

The General Board of Global Ministries responded reluctantly to an action of the 1980 General Conference that instructed the board to "devise appropriate structures to interpret and implement such opportunities for short-term volunteers in the global community." Two-and-a-half years later, the board set up an office with a part-time staff member, William Rollins. This was done through a committee in which practically no members had been personally involved with the volunteer movement. I did not see how such a plan could possibly work. My assumption has proven correct.

Rollins reports:

> My contributions were to bring national attention to this program and to have the College of Bishops of the Northeastern and Western Jurisdictions appoint jurisdictional coordinators. I have also encouraged every annual conference to appoint a VIM coordinator. I initiated periodic meetings with jurisdictional coordinators and sponsored joint finding trips to such places as Russia and Cuba as well as to the floods of the Midwest. Our work has emphasized the importance of VIM and contributed to a separate new structure of the General Board with a cabinet-level head.

Rollins served from 1984 until 1996. The head of the new Mission Volunteers unit, which includes UMVIM, is the Reverend Robert Walton, assisted by Jeanie Blankenbaker. His report reads, in part, as follows:

> The Christian church from its early beginnings has been about the business of calling persons to service, challenging them to put faith into action. The United Methodist Church has a strong tradition of personal piety and social responsibility. The women's missionary movement, which sprang up in the late 1800s, the United Methodist Committee on Relief begun in 1940, short-term volunteer service begun after World War II, all were the result of the church responding to societal needs and providing opportunities for service.
>
> In 1946 at the close of the war that devastated the world, the religious community came together to form the Commission on Voluntary Action and Service (name was later changed to Council of Religious Volunteer Agencies). Efforts were begun to rebuild war-torn areas, international youth exchanges were established, work camps were formed, and volunteers went throughout the world to begin acts of reconciliation. Several denominational volunteer programs trace their beginning to this time. Our own US-2s and 3s were born during this period. Young adults were challenged to give two years of volunteer service in this country, or three years working with mission projects in other countries, receiving only a small stipend for their service. Disaster

relief also gained momentum during this period, and UMCOR was calling hundreds of volunteers into service to provide relief.

For more than a century, Methodists have been reaching out to those in need in our communities through our church's mission institutions. Today hundreds of thousands of volunteers provide millions of hours working in soup kitchens, homeless shelters, abused women and children's programs, teaching literacy classes and English as a second language, and after-school tutoring. Local churches are creating all kinds of outreach ministries to the communities. In every way possible, these programs are volunteer-driven.

In addition to the annual and central conferences, which are organized geographically, the United Methodist Church has three missionary conferences and a language conference, which offer unique opportunities for volunteers. From their origin, the Alaska Missionary Conference, the Oklahoma Indian Missionary Conference, the Red Bird Missionary Conference, and the Rio Grande (Spanish-speaking) Conference have all invited volunteers, both individual and teams, to join with them in providing services to those in need. Volunteers have built churches and parsonages, taught vacation Bible school, joined in visitation campaigns, preaching missions, and youth camps.

Another SEJ mission agency with its unique involvement with volunteers is the SEJ Agency for Native American Ministries (SEJANAM). The Reverend Robert L. Mangum, director of the program at Lake Junaluska, tells not only of receiving work teams in their communities but of Native Americans busily sending their own committed church members as missionaries to other parts of the country and the world. Mangum reported that:

For three years straight we have been connecting Native Americans with indigenous Quechua and Aymara people of Bolivia. Native Americans have been coming home as missionaries, telling the story to non-Native-American churches and raising thousands of dollars for others. Stereotypes are broken and self-image is enhanced in the Native American community. They have sent work-team members to Africa University and individual volunteers to the Caribbean. One of my great recollections was the Prospect UMC work team, where I was pastor, that added a room and installed a bathroom for a paraplegic and his mother. A male skeptic non-believer was impressed that these folks were genuine Christians. They had been trying to win him for Christ, but their shovels and hammers and giving of money, time, and energy spoke loudest to his heart. Thank God for UMVIM!

Two much-beloved and respected mission institutions in the Southeast are the Red Bird Mission and Henderson Settlement, located in the mountains of eastern Kentucky. Both of these agencies are heavily dependent upon both short- and long-term volunteers in their schools and medical programs. In response to having received many teams over the years, Red Bird has taken upon itself the task of sending its own volunteers. According to one report, "eighty-five-year-old Essie Lamb says, 'It will be something I will never forget.'" She was one of twelve volunteers who went to Oklahoma Indian Missionary Conference (OIMC) to help the White Sand United Methodist Church congregation build a new sanctuary. The trip was step two in a dream to strengthen ties between the two missionary conferences. In 1996, the United Methodist Women of OIMC brought a team to the Red Bird Missionary Conference."

It should be noted here that most of the mission agencies cited above have done their own basic recruiting and placement of volunteers. UMVIM offices have sought to be supportive, especially in publicity and promotion.

Walton concluded:

Volunteer opportunities have experienced phenomenal growth in the last several years. Disaster relief following floods in the USA South and Midwest and hurricanes in the Caribbean, Louisiana, the two Carolinas, and Virginia have put volunteers to work for long periods of time. The Volunteers for Africa program, created in response to the call from the African church and guided by the leadership of Bishop Felton May, is involving volunteers from across the global church. Relief work in Bosnia, Herzegovina, and Croatia is utilizing hundreds of volunteers. These modern-day missionaries are also at work giving vital service and developing important contacts through the Russia Initiative. In cooperation with our ecumenical partners in the Council of Religious Volunteer Agencies, we are placing volunteers and providing technical assistance for the AmeriCorps program.

Ecumenical Partners

The UMVIM movement has developed and maintained close ties with a number of national and international ecumenical agencies. The first to be mentioned must be Habitat for Humanity, as it is so popular with our church members. Founder and President Millard Fuller has told me on more than one occasion that United Methodists make up a large portion of their volunteers. Though this is not surprising, it is certainly gratifying to know of that type of commitment by many volunteers in churches small or large, rural or urban.

Fuller said:

From the time John Wesley stood on tree stumps to preach the gospel to the poor, Methodists have been in ministry to their brothers and sisters in need. We are grateful that so many United Methodists are now looking to Habitat for Humanity to help them put their faith into action. In 1995 United Methodist congregations contributed $3,405,226 to HFH. The gifts of 3,556 congregations account for about 20 percent of our church support.

By way of example, of which there could be many, Millard reported, "After looking for a way that women could be in service to women, participants in the 1995 International United Methodist Women's Consultation funded and built a house in Atlanta. They were delighted to learn that the homeowner was a single woman with three children."

Another major ecumenical partner for UMVIM is Heifer Project International (HPI) with main offices in Little Rock, Arkansas. Organized in 1944 by the late Dan West, a compassionate Indiana farmer, this widely admired service agency is a non-profit program that, for over three decades, has provided farm animals and training in animal husbandry to low-income families in the USA and approximately one hundred other countries. The purpose of the project is to help small farmers produce protein food for themselves through more efficient use of natural resources. Distribution is made on the basis of need and ability to care for the gift. The key to HPI's success is that in each project the recipients agree to give an offspring of the original animal to another needy family. An HPI spokesman says that United Methodist volunteers have been very important to HPI from the very beginning and at many levels.

This wonderful ministry in its gift of animals program has grown steadily in Mexico, thanks in large measure to Terry and Muriel Henderson, United Methodist missionaries serving at the HPI center near Puebla. For a number of years before UMVIM was organized, the Hendersons had been busy placing volunteers, especially high school and college youth. Always these groups returned home with enthusiasm to share their stories of what they had learned, even in a couple of weeks.

Two of the most enthusiastic HPI supporters are volunteers Bill and Dorothy Appelgate of the Iowa Conference. This devoted couple was chosen by their peers to represent HPI at an awards ceremony at the White House, held to honor this leading volunteer organization.

A major ministry that has developed in our denomination around the issue of world hunger is the Harvest of Hope (HOH), founded by United Methodist ministers Ray Buchanan and Kenneth Horne, who felt called to salvage potatoes that were to be discarded and turn them over to food banks across the country and in other parts of the world. This program is sometimes referred to as the "potato project."

HOH staff members Julie Taylor and Susan Allen, at their national office in Big Island, Virginia, write:

> HOH brings together Christian persons who share the desire to *Do Something about Hunger* through gleaning. Many harvesters return to their own communities to reexamine lifestyle choices, especially in reducing waste of every kind. Some have shared that their relationship with God has been restored and service of this kind has drawn them closer to God. We encourage groups to distribute the gleaned produce in their own local areas to agencies in their community that work with the poor. In 1995 over 5,500 volunteers gleaned for others through the Gleaning Network.

Jubilee Partners of Comer, Georgia, is an ecumenical center that deals almost entirely with refugees from all over the world.

Volunteers have served as staff during the school year, assisting in teaching, translating, and enabling people unfamiliar with this country to develop skills by which they can adapt to a new environment. Many are political refugees who have been threatened with the lives of their families left at home. The personal contact between volunteers and refugees has been immensely rewarding. Other teams of volunteers have come to assist in the ever-growing building program. Another example of their concern for others can be found at Cenaporto, Nicaragua's prosthetics factory, on which the country's two thousand-plus amputees depend for arms and legs. Volunteers provide valuable service in this worthy cause. Don Mosley directs this important ministry.

The list of ecumenical agencies to which we relate could go on and on. But let me mention just one more, the Atlantic Street Center in Seattle. Kathleen Weber, US-2 and volunteer coordinator for the center, writes that this work was founded in 1910 as an Italian settlement house by two Methodist deaconesses. Today the social services focus on family comprehensive services. To help individual children and youth, one must include the whole family. "I have been impressed by the agency's use of volunteers. UMYF groups each spent one week this past year tutoring, chaperoning, caring for and helping low-income and homeless children. Two groups came from Washington while others were from Idaho and Colorado. The energy and hope that these teenagers bring is contagious and exciting. Hopefully we are able to provide an experience for them that challenges this idea of mission and their responsibility to the community."

One of the leading figures in volunteerism in our church, with a strong ecumenical thrust, is Melvin West of Missouri. He accelerated the development of work camps, as he likes to call them, for youth and adults. Mel maintains that

No needs exist in the world, but that God has provided the resources to meet those needs. There's not a hungry belly but there's a way to feed that person. There's not a leaky roof but there's somebody who can go and say, "I care for you" and really mean it. There's not a rotten porch but that somebody can rebuild it.

But he goes on to urge a word of caution. Mel declares, "You can patch all the roofs of the world, but if there is no love, you've only pounded nails."

Mel tells about a youth team sent to Hannibal, Missouri, to work on a shack unfit for human habitation. The house was made of scrap metal. The inside was cardboard boxes, flattened and nailed to the frame. A baby had frozen there the winter before. On the team was a junior-high-school girl in St. Louis. She and the others continued to learn from their new experiences. She said, "Brother West," and Mel said, "I thought she was going to say 'I don't ever want to come back here again,' but she said, 'Could you get Jodie and Ike, and we'll come back tomorrow?' Near the end of their time, this teenager said amidst her tears, 'Brother West, I will never complain about what I don't have.'" Her life was changed forever for the good.

The Commission on Religious Volunteer Agencies (CRVA) is the national ecumenical volunteer agency of which we have been a member since it was organized about ten years ago. We were also a member of its predecessor body. Representatives participate from the Church of the Brethren, Mennonite, Presbyterian, Lutheran, Baptist, Episcopal, and United Methodist denominations and occasionally from the Jewish community and the Roman Catholic Church and others. CRVA is a forum whereby ideas and concerns are shared with key volunteer leaders from different denominations. One interest has been to help with the placement of volunteers from another church, if the church being contacted does not have an appropriate opening at the time. United training seminars on voluntarism are also a key part of CRVA's work. This organization holds much promise for closer cooperation of interested churches, and indeed, is ecumenism in one of its finest forms.

Disaster Response

Coordinating volunteers serving on domestic projects has been Virginia Miller, based in Knoxville. She said, "United Methodists in Disaster Response is a combination of UMVIM and UMCOR. One without the other would be incomplete in its approach. So

UMVIM's energy, rebuilding skills, and willingness to go where needed are combined with UMCOR's expertise in helping the conferences and local communities to organize a recover agency." After Hurricane Hugo struck South Carolina with a vengeance, cooperation between the two agencies was quickly developed. Soon, the word came from the governor of South Carolina that, according to Virginia, "it was the M & M's of South Carolina who rebuilt our state, referring to the Methodists and the Mennonites!"

Virginia recalls an experience from Hurricane Fran on the North Carolina coast:

> A volunteer, in checking through a neighborhood, talked with an elderly lady who had twenty-five trees down in her yard. The lowest estimate for removing the trees was more than one hundred dollars per tree, and she did not have the funds. The volunteer said he had a youth group arriving over the weekend who would clear up the yard because they cared. The lady replied that youth were spoiled brats. She could not imagine that they would work, but slowly agreed to try. The youth came, and by noon on the first day, the same lady was proclaiming loudly that they are the most wonderful folks God ever made.

Nick Elliott, a pastor in the South Carolina Conference, has served as the Southeastern Jurisdiction UMVIM disaster response coordinator. Nick reported that

> for many years, United Methodist Volunteers In Mission have been a response arm of our church. When Hurricane Hugo hit South Carolina in September 1989, a new partnership between UMCOR and UMVIM began. UMCOR arrived in South Carolina to begin organizing response to Hugo and realized that UMVIM was a valuable agency for providing skilled labor and building knowledge to complete the response.

The current SEJ Disaster Response Coordinator for UMVIM–SEJ is Arthur Walker of Winter Haven, Florida. Elliott reported that

> six months after Hugo, a consultation between these two agencies was held in Memphis to consider closer cooperation in disaster response. Fred Toland

of Mobile, Alabama, was named as the liaison. At that time, he was the UMVIM-SEJ disaster response coordinator and on UMCOR staff. This arrangement worked well following Hurricane Andrew in Florida and Louisiana. A continued agreement worked with the south Georgia flood and numerous tornadoes. Several hurricanes hit the Caribbean islands and the US mainland in 1995. The agreement allowed us to respond in the Caribbean and with Hurricane Opal on the Gulf Coast. In 1996 hurricanes Bertha and Fran saw UMCOR organizing the response and UMVIM as the rebuilding agent.

When numerous churches were burned due to arson and racism in the Southeast and elsewhere, UMCOR approached the UMVIM-SEJ office to represent them in designing the United Methodist response. This action affirms UMCOR's belief in UMVIM's ability to respond well on their behalf during the time of disaster."

When Hurricane Andrew devastated the Miami area in 1995, the Miami district superintendent appointed Ann Burkholder and Lynette Fields to be in charge of The United Methodist Church's relief efforts. Their work for the next several years alleviated untold suffering and hardship. Jonathan Cloud, in an assessment of relief work, stated that "This denomination rose to the incredible task of entering into the disaster with nothing less than the God-given power to bring healing. What must never be forgotten is the fact that the Miami District persevered and struggled after becoming a 'wounded healer.' And this in my estimation is work done in the image of Christ."

Only days after the hurricane hit, Millard Fuller called to ask if we would cooperate with Habitat in the massive relief effort, focusing mostly on housing for those left stranded. His idea included joint sponsorship of the Manfred Retreat Center, which eventually provided accommodations and meals for most incoming volunteers.

One of the worst disasters to hit our country in recent years was the great flood that hit Albany and other parts of south Georgia in July 1994. The South Georgia Conference set up an 800-number telephone service staffed by volunteers Jim and Hilda Dutrow. By September, Bishop Richard C. Looney had appointed the Reverend Riley Middleton Jr., a member of the conference and a licensed contractor, to direct the rebuilding. He reported:

Volunteers In Mission became an important part of this effort. One of the vital elements in this type ministry is that it reaches beyond the mere construction of houses and takes on a very personal relationship between volunteer and flood survivor. The visiting volunteers became sympathetic listeners who gave people an outlet for their emotions related to the trauma. One woman in the disaster had been defrauded of almost all her money. When her house was rebuilt, she expressed gratitude and told how her faith in God had been renewed and her life turned in a new direction.

And while volunteers are on site, working especially in disaster-relief situations in which whole communities are involved, the denominational label is not so significant. Rich fellowship and bonding takes place, which hopefully will be carried back to one's local church. All across our country, the UMVIM movement has spread and developed in an utterly amazing way in response to desperate needs, including disaster-relief emergencies, without much of a national guideline to follow. This movement, under the Spirit of God, continues to expand to new areas of service and in different types of ministries. Thanks be to God for the Spirit which leads the way forward and thanks be to the volunteers who respond in God's name.

CHAPTER FOURTEEN

Around the World

Reports from Other Countries and Africa University

Where cross the crowded ways of life,
where sound the cries of race and clan,
above the noise of selfish strife,
we hear your voice, O Son of man.

Frank Mason North, 1903 (Matthew 22:9)

The world parish concept is a reality for countless volunteers who have traversed the globe in order to minister to human needs in the name of Jesus Christ. Nearly a hundred countries could be named of those who have hosted and shared with these servants of our Lord as they, together with their hosts, have grown in grace and faith.

The reports that follow are illustrative of the many ministries carried out by volunteers. Many have shared their stories with me, but space limitations simply will not allow for much recall. I am deeply grateful to all who have shared their experiences with me in the preparation of this book. My regret is that we could include only a representative few. The reports are listed by continent or geographical region. This is not intended to be a comprehensive review, but to illustrate the work being done.

Africa

Africa University. The General Conference of the United Methodist Church of 1988 authorized the establishment of the first institution of higher education by our denomination on the continent of Africa. This project has become in the minds of many church leaders the single most important mission project ever undertaken by United Methodists and is supported by churches and individuals from all across the globe.

But to begin such an enormous task without adequate funds, buildings, staff, or students seemed to be an impossible situation. Plus the fact that the Zimbabwean president was reluctant at first to grant a charter for what would become the first private university in that country. An excellent site had been chosen by the selection committee headed by Dr. James Laney of Emory University. With a strong denominational base and a stable society in an English-speaking population, this choice was quite a natural one.

In mid 1991, I received a call from Dr. John W. Z. Kurewa, head of the proposed university. He was asking if our office could recruit and send work teams to the site in order to renovate some old buildings that had fallen into disrepair and make them into classrooms, offices, library, and other facilities. I gladly accepted his request and put out the word across the country. All five jurisdictions sent at least one team, which enabled the campus to open as planned on March 22, 1992. Only a few weeks before, the president of Zimbabwe signed the bill authorizing the charter. He said that decision was made due to the fact that our church had demonstrated its seriousness in the sending of teams. Dr. Kurewa has often cited the critical help that UMVIM gave in the very beginning of Africa University.

In 1993 another call came from Dr. Kurewa asking help from teams in the construction of staff housing on the campus to save the cost of rental property in the nearby city of Mutare. Several of those have been finished and are occupied. Others are in the planning stage. The UMVIM office in Atlanta is coordinating all arrangements for groups wanting to serve on this project.

The First United Methodist Church in Pittsburgh has sponsored a chemical engineer who has spent his career starting up chemical and power-plant projects. The initial enthusiasm of this church has continued ever since. Jim Crossley said that his call to mission became quite clear upon hearing Bishop Roy Nichols tell of the needs of the university. Jim said:

Lord, if agriculture students should know something about irrigation pumps and piping, maybe I can be of some use. After correspondence with AU officials and a few calls to the Atlanta office, I was about to be on my way to a country that, in my ignorance of Africa, I had to find on the map. In all my start-up experience there has been nothing to match the excitement of helping to start a brand-new university in a developing country for students from all of Africa.

Angola. Since this country is Portuguese-speaking, only a limited number of volunteers have been able to serve, usually former missionaries to Angola or Mozambique, or persons who have learned Portuguese from another source. Volunteers have often been individuals or couples spending from several months up to a year and include medical personnel, technicians, accountants, and other specialists. A few building teams have helped with important construction projects.

Ghana. As a former district of the British Methodist Conference, Ghana has long welcomed UMVIM volunteers. These have usually served in some type of building or agricultural program as well as in the field of teaching. Coordination of volunteers has been handled by Charles and Patty Maddox, former UMVIM volunteers and now missionaries of our church from Kentucky.

Kenya. This church gained its independence from British Methodism years ago and has frequently welcomed volunteers from other countries. They have served mainly at the Maua Methodist Hospital, both in teams and as individuals. Teams have also gone to help with construction of the Kenya Methodist University (not to be confused with Africa University, the United-Methodist-related university in Zimbabwe designed to serve the whole African continent).

Liberia. Due to continuing civil conflict, volunteers have been quite few. When conditions allow, a goodly number go to serve, particularly in teaching, building, and medical work.

Mozambique. Like Angola, this is a Portuguese-speaking country and receives only a few volunteers. Similarly, most have been former missionaries back to serve in hospitals, schools, or agricultural programs, or in the conference office for several months up to a year or longer.

Sierra Leone. Due to warring conditions here, visitors have been discouraged, though several have done outstanding and much-needed work.

Southern Africa. Here the work is in coordination with the Methodist Church of Southern Africa, which, in addition to South

Africa, includes several surrounding countries. UMVIM's main contribution has been in sending building teams to help erect church facilities. The church established its own program in 1992, called Southern Africa Methodist Volunteers In Mission (SAMVIM). That same year their Methodist conference asked Richard Bosart to serve as the first director of volunteer mission work. Bosart had been greatly influenced for mission service by the late Dr. David Flude, a British Methodist missionary and former UMCOR staff member. Many important projects have already been completed through SAMVIM's effort, with more on the way.

Uganda. As a new place of ministry for United Methodism, Uganda has welcomed volunteers who have sought to help in a variety of ministries. Linda Griffith of Kentucky has been the principal coordinator of these teams. Kathy and Mark Masters were assigned by GBGM to Uganda as coordinators of volunteer services, but political disturbances have curtailed their work.

Zaire, Rwanda, and Burundi. Here also, civil disorder at times has disrupted the flow of volunteers. Yet some of the most important work done by volunteers has been in providing emergency care for the multitudes of refugees in this vast area. Judy Neal, RN of Lexington, Kentucky, is one who has given of herself untiringly in ministering to the victims of war and genocide.

Zimbabwe. With a strong base in our denomination and a stable society in an English-speaking population, this country is one of the most popular outside the US for volunteers. Africa University alone attracts several dozen teams and individuals each year. The main goals at AU thus far have been to renovate old abandoned farm buildings into the first classrooms and offices in readiness for its opening in 1992, and to build up to twelve houses on the campus for staff members. Volunteer teachers have been useful in the various colleges and library. The Zimbabwe Annual Conference has also received a fair number of teams helping on new church buildings and conducting pastoral seminars and other special programs.

Asia/Pacific

Australia. The Uniting Church in Australia has been host to a small number of individual volunteers. These have been young adults who have served approximately one year in various fields of social service. One was able to conduct a thorough research project on behalf of one of the church councils, on the subject of family abuse.

Hong Kong. Volunteers have been taken to this hub of Southeast Asia by Dr. Kenneth and Iweeta McIntosh of Dallas, who spent many years of service there. They themselves have been very much involved in helping the church prepare for the momentous change when the island reverted to Chinese control. Ken reported:

> The first volunteer study/work team was held in 1995 with the Methodist Church in various sites of Hong Kong, Kowloon, and the Portuguese colony of Macau. Emphasis was placed on helping youth considered "at risk" in that they do not have academic skills necessary to be placed in their age group in schools and are in danger of becoming social dropouts. Another was related to the care of the home-bound and elderly. In addition, we worked with many of the thousands of children, youth, and adults who are mentally challenged. The volunteer program in Hong Kong and Macau is different from the more traditional idea of service as builders or medical personnel. It is a "people experience" in learning and sharing.

India. One of our UMVIM leaders in the Southeast is Dr. Solomon Christian, originally from India, who practices dentistry in Memphis, Tennessee. He and others from our office have had encouraging consultations with bishops of the church in India, and a number of teams have followed. The distance and cost discourage many from making such a trip.

Indonesia. Though Protestants are in a small minority, Methodism is strong and the church has invited volunteers to join in their ministry. Only a small number have thus far been able to respond, but they report a most meaningful experience with the people.

The Philippines. The key person in the Southeast who has helped to open the door to our work in this country is the Reverend Jim Mishoe of the South Carolina Conference. Through a long friendship with Philippine church leaders, Jim has gained their confidence; and many groups have gone to help on some major building projects.

Caribbean

Antigua. This island is where the headquarters of the Methodist Church in the Caribbean and the Americas is located, and is also the area where more volunteers have served outside the US than any other part of the world. Note that this area includes Central America as well as the Caribbean proper. Reports will be shared on a country-by-country basis.

Bahamas. Smaller numbers of volunteers have gone to this island due to its higher living standards. However, important contributions have been made following hurricanes and in providing volunteer pastoral services.

Belize and Honduras. Belize has received large numbers of teams, mainly on church and school construction. Honduras, as a Spanish-speaking country, has had fewer teams, but significant work has been done with the Methodist Church and in ecumenical activity. Another major partner with us in Honduras has been the Christian Council for Development with Naomi Espinoza and Tim Wheeler in various phases of the work with the poor all over the country.

Guyana. Though at the northern tip of South America, Guyana touches Caribbean waters and so is a part of the MCCA. Founded by British Methodists, the church has been desperate for emergency assistance in renovations and repairs to which many groups have responded. UMVIM coordinators for Guyana, Global Ministries personnel Bill and Diana Upchurch, report,

> This movement continues to provide hope for the people in Guyana, building churches, outreach centers, church offices, libraries, retreat centers, vacation Bible school, worship, and other services. Most of all, they have brought themselves! They have worked at our side, slept in our homes and eaten at our tables. This ministry is a living example of our oneness in the body of Christ and our world-wide Methodist connection.

Haiti. Often referred to as the poorest nation in the Western Hemisphere, Haiti has probably received per capita more volunteers than any other country in the world. Our hosts there are extremely gracious and welcoming, despite their severely limited resources. Hundreds of churches, parsonages, schools, clinics, and other facilities have been added due to the work of volunteers. While not knowing the local language is a handicap, people find some way to communicate and share and grow together. A good number of volunteers have received their call to the ministry while on a team to Haiti or upon their return.

Haiti received a big boost in its effort to get more UMVIM teams with the appointment of the first volunteer coordinators, Charles and JoAnn Selph from Florida. The Haitian Methodist Superintendent, the Reverend Allan Kirton, had asked Bishop Joel McDavid to send the Selphs to speed up the flow of teams with persons assigned for the particular task of helping make all the necessary arrangements. They gave of themselves most whole-heartedly and are dearly loved by the people. Charles writes:

Of the many joys we hold dear of our years in Haiti, the most precious have to do with people—both Haitians and work-team members—and God's faithfulness! It was not uncommon to see conversions taking place among team members as well as renewed commitments to Christ as they shared his love together. The team members seemed always to be impressed with the faith of the Haitian Christians. It was plain to see they were rich in spirit, a powerful testimony that made a definite impact on volunteers.

When the Selphs had to leave due to medical problems, the next coordinators were missionaries Betty and Allen Darby of Canada, who added the task of coordinating teams of volunteers to their usual schedule. They also greatly endeared themselves to the local people, becoming effective in their use of Creole. Betty likes to recall:

Memories—yes—we have lots of those because we received many teams in Petit-Goave during 1973–79 and in Jeremie, 1979–84. Most of our memories are positive. We remember Haitians and Americans working and worshiping side by side; some team members sharing their "life-changing experience" with them; trying to cut expenses for the teams to the bone; local people providing materials and transport into inaccessible places; North Carolinians who thought *tea* meant *iced tea*; the prayers of thanksgiving of people who had prayed for sometimes as long as ten years for a church building. It was exhausting at times hosting all these folk—and trying to have the building sites ready for them. The results in those days were often spectacular. If the foundations were ready in advance, a team would put up the walls in ten-plus days, hold their closing worship in the new church, and local people would complete the work after the team left.

The next full-time coordinators for Haiti were Bill and Cecelia Manness, who were supported by the Western North Carolina Conference. Again, they were dearly loved by the people and appreciated for their ability to communicate in Creole. Health reasons forced them to retire. Other coordinators have been Benny and Linda Neal, and Nancy Osgood.

The Reverend Moise L. D. Isidore, president of the Haiti District of the Methodist Church, has expressed his appreciation of the work of so many UMVIM teams. He has written to indicate that from 1982 to 1997, completed projects with volunteer personnel include twenty-two churches, eleven schools, and eight multi-purpose buildings. But he stressed most the

transformation of people's lives. Let me give one practical example of a blind beggar in Petit-Goave some fourteen years ago. A surgical team came from Texas and operated on this man, who recovered his sight. Then he became an active member of the Petit-Goave Church. Through the interaction between UMVIM and Haitians, many, many lives have been touched and transformed. Team members have often declared that they are not the same since they have visited Haiti, and several have joined the ministry.

So many volunteer teams have served in Haiti and remained faithful with their support over a number of years. One such person is Joe Cal Watson of Ridge Springs, South Carolina. Joe and his brother, Mike, went together to Haiti some years ago. As an agriculturist and lover of people, Joe was caught up in the situation and has since poured his heart into helping develop a strong agricultural program through the church. He and others have annually sponsored some Haitian young people to attend college in this country. No one I know has demonstrated a more consistent and creative support to the people of Haiti than Joe Cal Watson.

Jamaica. The largest of the eight districts of the MCCA, Jamaica has also received among the highest number of volunteers. A massive relief effort was underway in 1985 following the devastation of Hurricane Gilbert. This simply added to the already crushing need. Medical volunteers have also been very active at several hospitals across the country. The Methodist Church in Jamaica organized its own medical committee to direct this ministry. Our chief hosts here have been the Reverend Katherine Gale and the Reverend Claude Cadogan, along with many pastors and local church people.

Leeward Islands. This group of islands has had more than its share of hurricanes. Many teams have gone to assist in the emergency relief efforts as well as in regular, much-needed church construction projects. Several ministers have shared in pastoral leadership, counseling, and evangelism.

Panama/Costa Rica. These two countries work as one district, and each has received many teams. In Panama, special attention has been given to aiding the Quaymi Indians with two foot-bridges in the jungle where rivers become uncrossable in the rainy season. This unique operation included bringing in a helicopter to help deliver heavy supplies that could not be brought in by any other means. Leadership for this highly skilled effort came from Dr. Lester Spencer of the Alabama/West Florida Conference. Another major effort in Panama was to replace a large number of houses destroyed by the United States military invasion of Panama, and all jurisdictions sent teams to help. Key leadership for this project came from Glenn Abernathy of the Tennessee Conference. Our work in both countries has been with the two sister Methodist denominations, one originally from the US and the other from Britain. Bishop Pedro Araüz of the Evangelical Methodist Church of Panama has written to express his appreciation for those who have come "to serve with us in a show of solidarity and love for those who are poor and weak."

Windward Islands. Located in the South Caribbean area, these islands include St. Vincent, Grenada, and smaller islands. Teams have helped build churches, a Christian education center and a parsonage, as well as repairing and adding to existing structures. Large medical teams led by Dr. James and Linda Fields of Nashville have served in St. Vincent annually since 1984 caring for the medically underserved in the more rural areas. Several children have been brought to the United States for life-transforming surgery not yet available in their home country.

Cuba. At the General Conference of 1992, I spoke to Cuba's Methodist Bishop Joel Ajo about our interest in the possibility of sending volunteers to share in ministry with his church. He assured me that they would be welcomed. An investigating team was sent down from our office to confer with him and other leaders. Upon contacting government authorities, we learned that they were skeptical as to our main reason for wanting to come to Cuba. Finally a senior official agreed that one team could come, and said that this group would be watched constantly. So we selected an experienced, mature team to be the first to make the visit. As their work on a church facility was nearing completion, the volunteers noticed that government workers on a nearby project needed more help. So, as the team finished its commitment at the church, it moved on to join the government workers on their project. Word of this incident reached the official most concerned, and he responded with amazement. He further said that we should feel free to bring all such groups. Prior to 1990, Methodist buildings were almost falling apart, as no construction materials were available for repairs. In the early 1990s the situation changed, and we have maintained a flow of teams for several years with groups scheduled often a year or more in advance.

Dominican Republic. This Spanish-speaking country bordered by Haiti has been the recipient of many teams working with the Evangelical Church of the Dominican Republic. This church is a merger of former Methodist, Presbyterian, and Moravian churches. For the past several years, the Presbyterian Church has had a full-time coordinator on hand to help guide this growing work, the first being Anna Callison, then Penny Diehl, and now the Reverend Benjamin and Shannon Langley. They all report extremely helpful volunteers working on all types of programs and projects.

Puerto Rico. Volunteer coordinator the Reverend Miriam Visot gives a glowing report of vast numbers of individual and team volunteers who have served across the island. Most have been engaged in church building projects, and others in special programs for children and youth.

Central America

Costa Rica. As in Panama, Methodism is represented by both former American and British branches, the former known as the Evangelical Methodist Church of Costa Rica and the other as part of the MCCA Panama/Costa Rica District. In the Evangelical Methodist Church, volunteer work has been widespread throughout the entire country. A request came to our office for a gifted evangelist who was fluent in Spanish. The Reverend Ted Grout of the Rio Grande Conference responded to this appeal. He and a number of others have been active in conducting evangelism campaigns and seminars for pastors. The Evangelical Methodist Church of Costa Rica has received a large number of construction teams, many with experience in evangelism and Christian education.

Ecuador. Despite only a small Methodist following, their leaders have invited volunteers to come and join with their ministry. Much of the focus has been on one large multi-purpose Christian center.

El Salvador. Though without a strongly organized Methodist presence, volunteer work, mostly construction and evangelism, has proceeded in cooperation with the Baptist church and ecumenical bodies.

Guatemala. Here the Evangelical Methodist Church has warmly welcomed many teams in a wide variety of opportunities for service. Ecumenical agencies and the Moravian Church have also been our hosts where construction and medical teams are providing emergency services.

Honduras. As Honduras is a Spanish-speaking country with limited Methodist presence, few volunteers have worked here, but significant work has been carried on with both the Belize-Honduras District of the MCCA and the Christian Council for Development, with Naomi Espinoza and Tim Wheeler, and the Heifer Project International program, all working across the poorest parts of the country. Many building and teaching teams have ministered in the English-speaking Bay Islands off the coast of Honduras.

Mexico. About 1977 I made my first official visit to Mexico and conferred with Bishop Ulises Hernandez. He seemed rather perplexed and kept asking me why I had come. My response was simply to say I wanted to learn about the work of the Methodist Church. I never mentioned our interest in sharing ministry during that first discussion. He sent me out to a rural area for a few days, and then invited me to come back and attend a Cabinet meeting. There one of the district superintendents told me my visit was too short, and that I must come back. The bishop concurred, and furthermore asked me to bring other colleagues. In about five months we were back and shared in an excellent orientation session about the church and the country and its culture. Those accompanying me represented about ten annual conferences of the SEJ. They returned home to promote the projects they had seen. Since then, hundreds of teams have gone to serve, thanks to this good start.

My first contact with any volunteer coordinators was with Terry and Muriel Henderson of the Heifer Project International program located at Puebla. They had already been hosting teams and developing opportunities for many youth and adult teams. Perhaps the person who has given more time to the coordinating process than any other is Marianne Hutchinson, who was based in Monterrey. Her easy use of Spanish greatly simplified all the arrangements that had to be worked out. A few years ago I was asked to meet with all six bishops (three having just been added) to discuss this ministry. Each bishop brought a volunteer coordinator to that meeting, which again strengthened our relationships.

All the Mexican bishops have been strongly supportive of our work together, most of them having been invited here for some of our training programs. Bishop Raul Ruiz has been one of our keenest supporters. He reports:

Yes, I affirm that the greatest blessing UMVIM teams have brought cannot be evaluated in terms of numbers or material goods. For us Christians there are no borders nor cultural and linguistic barriers to prevent us from serving people in the name of our Lord Jesus Christ. Neither can unjust political or economic policies established by humans stop us from sharing with others, like our brothers and sisters from Cuba who have been suffering a non-Christian and genocidal economic embargo for more than thirty years. We have learned many things in our ministry together with UMVIM, to be responsible even though some people have little material goods compared to others, and the important thing is how you share what you have. While we sometimes think the only thing we have to do is give, it is important to be open to receive. This giving and receiving enriches life for those who participate in these dynamics. This is, to me, what UMVIM is all about, and I praise God for it!

Nicaragua. For the last several decades, volunteers have been serving primarily with the Moravian Church in its strong medical program and other outreach ministries. Our ministry here has also been with ecumenical agencies like CEPAD, under the direction of Catalina Diaz, which works with the poorest of the poor and with other Christian organizations. As a victim of US negligence after the civil war and unfulfilled promises by our country, Nicaragua continues to suffer grave economic problems. Volunteers have helped by providing building skills and medical services, providing assistance in agricultural programs, and teaching English.

Europe and the Middle East

Armenia. This small country once under Russian control is struggling to stand on its own feet. Only a limited number of volunteers have been able to go there, but plans are underway to increase our participation in the life of the church. The Western North Carolina and Oklahoma Conferences are presently among those sending volunteers.

Bosnia. The civil disorder and violence that have rocked this country have made it a rather dangerous place to serve. However, dedicated volunteers have been at work in several important ministries, particularly in caring for children and youth.

Estonia, Latvia, and Lithuania. These three Balkan countries have a long history of Methodism and have enjoyed the fellowship and service of a number of specialized teams. The biggest project has been the Agape United Methodist Center, which includes a seminary being built in the Estonian city of Parnu to serve much of Europe and Russia. Two of the primary coordinators for volunteer work in Estonia are Nancy Eubanks and John Trundle.

Bishop Hans Vaxby of the Northern Europe Central Conference has written to express his appreciation for

two construction experts from Illinois, Leonard Land and Aaron Kram, who together with their wives came all the way to Latvia in 1993. They came at their own expense. They came to climb every roof, dive into every cellar, and investigate every corner of the four buildings in Riga and Liepaja that we, at that point, had hoped to get back from the state.

Their commitment showed me what love for the Kingdom of God means, and what it is to be a part of the Methodist connection. After that, I have seen dozens of teams and thousands of footprints after them in Estonia, Latvia, and Lithuania. UMVIM has given faith, hope, and love to our church in the Baltic countries with an impact that reaches far beyond our national borders.

Under Bishop Vaxby's leadership, the Baltic Mission Center is being rebuilt in Tallin with the help of UMVIM teams. The original church was the first Methodist-owned facility in Riga. It had been the largest Methodist congregation in Northern Europe, and is now preparing church leaders for the Balkan countries and Russia.

Germany. Prior to the unification of Germany, Robin Harp of Atlanta's Peachtree Road United Methodist Church with the United Methodist Women in East Germany provided services for refugees who were being abused in different ways. She was highly commended for her efforts by church leaders.

Palestine/Israel. This hot spot on the world map is drawing an increasing number of volunteers who work closely with the Middle East Council of Churches and the United Methodist missionaries in the area. Bonnie Jones Gehweiler of Lake Junaluska, North Carolina, has been the principal coordinator of teams to Palestine. Her hope is that more Americans can have first-hand contact with Palestinian Christians who are being severely persecuted and restricted by Israel.

Russia and Other Territories. Well over several thousand volunteers have been at work in Russia and surrounding territories since the collapse of the Soviet Union. Many have gone to help renovate and repair damaged and neglected structures of the Russian Orthodox Church. Some have helped with United Methodist programs such as prayer meetings, church services, and teaching English. Others have helped establish Methodist fellowships and congregations, and have renovated orphanages and health-treatment centers.

Wales. A former missionary couple to Jamaica, the Reverend Stephen and Myrtle Poxon have hosted a number of volunteers, both teams and individuals, in their demanding urban ministry in the city of Cardiff. They have served as counselors and teachers, helping young people confront and overcome difficult circumstances in their lives.

South America

Bolivia. The Methodist Evangelical Church of Bolivia has long been receiving many teams in their vast ministry across the country. This has included a heavy emphasis on volunteer medical personnel at the Methodist Hospital, in church building projects, in agricultural programs, and in the teaching of English. Retired missionaries Ruth Ann Robinson of Texas and Bob and Rosa Caufield of North Alabama have hosted many groups and individuals. This work is now being coordinated by Dakin Cook of North Georgia.

Brazil. The Methodist Church in Brazil with its seven regions is attracting many volunteers. As a result of a consultation held several years ago between the UMVIM-SEJ Office and their bishops, a decision was made to name one person as their national coordinator for all volunteers. The bishops appointed the Reverend James Goodwin, a missionary from the North Alabama Conference, to this post. Since then, much additional involvement has taken place. This includes not only building projects, but vacation Bible schools for children, adult training seminars, teaching English, and other special programs. Of special interest has been the decision by the Brazilian Methodists to establish a medical fellowship for medical personnel, known as "Evangemed," to provide volunteers in medical and evangelistic outreach to the poor.

The World Methodist Council has joined with the Methodist Church of Brazil to establish a mobile medical/dental clinic which serves the poor of the Rio de Janeiro area and other parts of Brazil, providing health care and proclaiming the Gospel. The clinic is directed by Dr. Wilson Bonfim, and staffed with full-time health care workers and evangelists from Brazil, and volunteers from Brazil and the United States. Dr. James Fields served as a consultant assisting the Brazilian Methodists in developing a volunteer medical mission program and encouraging volunteerism among the Brazilian health professionals.

Chile. This independent Methodist Church has been another to welcome volunteers who have served in many of the ministries of their church. The Reverend Flor Rodriguez is the present volunteer coordinator, the previous coordinator having been Florrie Snow.

Colombia. This new Methodist Church is now open to volunteers, and it is expected that many will go there to serve. The coordinator is the Reverend Luis Castiblanco.

Venezuela. This country has also recently started Methodist work and is inviting teams to help in church construction. In addition, Servants in Faith and Technology, a missionary training agency in the North Alabama Conference, is sending groups to help build a training facility near Caracas for use by Latin Americans in their home areas.

A number of other countries have also received volunteers, both as teams and as individuals. And the number of participants and countries involved keeps growing each year. In addition to hosting construction and medical volunteers, a number of countries are now sending their own, either to the same country or other places. The numbers of participants seem to be increasing constantly.

CHAPTER FIFTEEN

Into the Future

What Lies Ahead for UMVIM

"Go, make of all disciples." We welcome thy command.
"Lo, I am with you always." We take thy guiding hand.
The task looms large before us; we follow without fear;
In heaven and earth thy power shall bring God's kingdom here.

Leon M. Adkins, 1955

Christian volunteers have been around as long as the Christian church. Over the years there have been many types of volunteer service, and we do well to keep them in mind when considering the future. The past with its achievements and disappointments will help mold the years yet to be.

Dr. Joe Hale, general secretary of the World Methodist Council, addressed one of the first UMVIM rallies about the way "the God of the whole world calls Christians to mission." He quoted Dr. Emilio Castro of Uruguay, who said, "The end of the missionary era is at hand. Now we are in the time of the world mission of the church." Hale and Castro were pointing to the changing scene in the Christian world in which people of all lands are considered the "mission field," a concept that is becoming well known to UMVIM participants everywhere.

At the 1976 Southeastern Jurisdictional Conference, the Volunteers In Mission movement was officially recognized for the first time. Since then, UMVIM has had tremendous growth all across the country, due mainly to its emphasis upon grassroots leadership and participation. Each jurisdiction now has its own director or coordinator, though most are either part-time or voluntary. Only UMVIM-SEJ at this time has a staff of several full-time workers, and has had such since 1979. A few conferences now have full-time coordinators, and others are considering doing the same.

In the beginning, this movement was not well received by many mission leaders. Critics complained of racism, sexism, classism and lack of adequate preparation and orientation. Those of us in leadership positions have been quick to acknowledge these shortcomings while at the same time affirming the tremendous potential of volunteer service. As the movement has gained momentum through the shared experiences of participants, it has become a source of renewal in the lives of many individuals and congregations. A wave of acclamation from leaders across the entire church is being experienced.

Questions come often to those of us who serve this cause. Why has this grassroots movement become so popular? Why have so many persons decided to participate in this form of mission service? Will the excitement continue indefinitely? I would like to suggest a few reasons I believe interest in voluntary mission service will continue for many years to come.

First, UMVIM is complementary to other forms of mission service. It affirms the traditional mission concept and seeks to work in partnership with career missionaries. But administratively, UMVIM is under the direction of local annual conference personnel and the host country or community's church leaders without control by a central mission agency.

Second, UMVIM places the emphasis on personal involvement in a hands-on ministry that has great emotional appeal. All persons have skills and talents to share. The hands-on mission work being undertaken by United Methodist Men, for example, clearly illustrates its appeal to laymen of the church. Teams are often intergenerational, offering a setting where teenagers and retirees work side by side as they share gifts in ministry.

Third, the emphasis is not on raising large sums of money. While most volunteers contribute funds to assist projects with which they are associated, fundraising is not UMVIM's primary focus. One overseas leader takes the position of never asking the visiting group for a specific contribution. He accepts whatever they can bring, again with the emphasis on having people present who can both give and receive. Promotion for Advance Special projects is handled, in the main, by other programs in the church rather than by teams or individuals. Volunteers make significant contributions, however, for the Advance projects to which they are related.

Fourth, the UMVIM ministry opens possibilities for mission service to people in all walks of life and from different economic, social, and educational levels. It affirms the sanctity and uniqueness of all persons in their quest for an opportunity to serve the Lord.

Fifth, volunteers are responsible for their own expenses. They are not a drain on the church budget, even if their church decides to help them. They receive no salary and are dependent upon their own resources for travel and other personal expenses.

Sixth, volunteers work in full partnership with their hosts, whether here or in other countries. They go in response to an official invitation. Visitors and hosts work together in a mutual manner. For many people, especially abroad, this sense of mutuality in mission represents a new day in Christian mission.

Seventh, volunteers are very mobile and quick to respond to emergency situations, here and abroad. United Methodists are always present in significant numbers when hurricanes, tornadoes, earthquakes, and other disasters occur.

Eighth, and last, UMVIM celebrates the thousands of persons who readily testify that their volunteer service has changed their lives. Christ's call to them has become quite real. They are no longer the same. They return home as renewed and dedicated church members, more eager to share in the work of their local church and to tell their story of what God is doing in another part of the world.

As an active medical volunteer, Linda Fields of Nashville, Tennessee, illustrates the above in an article in *New World Outlook* mission magazine:

> One cannot measure the impact of a VIM mission experience on a team but must reflect on the effect of the experience on individual team members. But how can one evaluate the impact on a patient or team member when an ulcer finally heals? Or when a once-deformed child thanks his doctor for

making him so handsome? Or when sight is restored and the patient shouts praises to God? Our lives and the lives of many Vincentians have been transformed, and we are the richer for having been in each other's presence, knowing that God is in the midst of it all. (*New World Outlook* [New York: General Board of Global Ministries, 1995], 18-19)

By all means we must face the future with eyes wide open. This will mean we must encounter problems and limitations of the volunteer movement with patience and resolve. According to pastor and sociologist Phil Amerson of Evansville, Indiana, "The emergence of the volunteer phenomenon suggests a redistribution of resources and power as well as new linkages in the way communities and societies function. Volunteerism also suggests a freedom on the part of persons to act in new ways." One danger he cites is that of a "paratrooper approach, where people drop in from out of the sky, leaving when their work is ended; even so, volunteerism must not be truncated or isolated from other more structured change-focused efforts."

The Reverend Allan Kirton, director of the GBGM Mission Resource Center in Atlanta, raises serious questions as to how volunteers with a concern for Haiti, for example, ought to respond in the future. He advocates identifying with the poor—"using our resources, prestige and influence to benefit the poor, and opening ourselves up to be saved from the arrogance and insensitivity which military might and financial strength often confer."

Chief staff executive for GBGM mission personnel office, the Reverend John McCullough, is almost effusive in describing the impact of this movement. He said:

Toward the latter decades of the twentieth century, volunteerism has become an important source of transformation for The United Methodist Church. An unexpected new reality, volunteerism has been like the deep inhaling of fresh morning air, inflating the lungs, urging the breath of new life to come in and go forth. These volunteers have demonstrated the power of faith when it is accompanied by action. Therein resides new life for both the giver and the receiver for each act of kindness. Unspeakable joy is the refrain that follows volunteer efforts in whatever service is done.

Mr. McCullough pointed out that volunteerism can be risky business:

> First, it can make one vulnerable. Cultural exchanges and attempts to complete tasks with available resources can have a profound impact on the way in which one views the world and understands God's activity and purpose. Second, it can make one frustrated, even angry. Being exposed to people whose lives are caught in cycles of despair and poverty, and building relationships with them can disturb one's sense of inner peace and personal fulfillment. Third, it can make one change direction in life. Expressions of appreciation for the volunteer's presence and the need for continuing involvement can alter the focus of one's value system and sense of priority.

Mr. McCullough expressed the hope that "such stories will inform one's faith, and inspire greater participation in the movement."

To consider the future for the volunteer movement is to ask a number of hard questions about life on this planet we call home. Think of the enormity of confronting global warming, overpopulation, genetic testing, inhuman conditions for the vast majority of the population, and a host of other issues. What difference can UMVIM be expected to make in light of these overwhelming concerns?

Help can come from such leaders as theologian Donald E. Messer, whose book, *A Conspiracy of Goodness,* speaks of many changes that must be made for mission as we move into the next century. He claims:

> Humanity is poised over the epicenter of a global earthquake, but remains oblivious to the damage being inflicted to God's creation and obtuse to the danger of the extinction of all life. . . . When the rain forests burn in the Amazon, an ozone hole opens in the atmosphere, or nuclear weapons [or land mines] proliferate among the nations, complacent apathy prevails.... Theology, mission, and ministry must move beyond rigid past boundaries and help shape a global environment for future generations. ([Nashville: Abingdon Press, 1992], 24)

The missionary of the future will represent more of the

> global nature of Christianity.... Nearly 90 percent of all the world's missionaries for the past two hundred years have come from Europe and North America.... Today Two-Thirds World churches send over twenty thousand missionaries to other peoples. (pp. 35-36)

The volunteer movement must somehow acknowledge and relate to this new fact of our time. It will be an enormous challenge to merge the vast numbers of volunteers into a team working together with thousands of missionaries from quite different backgrounds.

> Too few North Americans possess the cross-cultural expertise for communicating the gospel. Many remain unaware of their own social "baggage," unable to separate cultural mores from Christian morals, and unwilling to acknowledge their own complicity in evil social structures.... Can we truly renounce our luxuries and embrace poverty? ... To what degree can we suffer with our sisters and brothers in Christ? (p. 55)

It is estimated that American Christians keep for themselves 98 percent of their income and donate the remaining two percent to church causes. Of that amount, only about 20 percent will go to mission programs in the United States or other countries. How will UMVIM change or even influence this way of doing the Lord's business?

A major point for the years ahead, according to Messer, is that "no missional issue may divide evangelical and ecumenical Christians more than the question of interfaith dialogue and relationships" (*A Conspiracy of Goodness*, 136). Again the question arises, How does the volunteer deal with such an issue, simply by ignoring it or trying to come to terms with an issue that may be outside one's daily routine, but of critical importance in cross-cultural relations?

Without doubt we live in a changing world for Christian mission, vastly different even from that of recent years. Researchers tell us that more than two billion of the earth's peoples remain cut off from Christian churches and missionaries. Of this number, refugees world-wide make up a staggering fourteen to eighteen million people and the number seems only to increase.

One of the most influential and creative leaders in this movement is the Reverend John T. Martin Jr., who served as president of the UMVIM-SEJ Board of Directors for eight years. He had this to say about what lies ahead for us:

> God has been opening doors for the UMVIM movement on every continent and in many lands where doors have been closed until recently. Only God knows where the future will take us, but we know who holds the future. Let it be enough for us to continue heeding God's beckoning Spirit in faith that God is working and so must we. Whether we be senders or receivers or hopefully both, Christ is in our midst with the words of life. May we find our lives as we put Christian love in action.

Reaching persons not yet touched for Jesus Christ is one of the greatest challenges confronting the volunteer movement. This reminds us once again of a term used prominently decades ago and referred to as "the unfinished task." Dr. Tracey Jones, retired mission chief executive, said, "The challenges confronting the churches are so massive, so complex, so critical, that anything less than the response of the whole membership will not be adequate to meet them. Every Christian must see himself or herself as a missionary of Jesus Christ confronting people in the no-man's land between faith and unbelief" (*Our Mission Today* [New York: World Outlook Press, 1963], 126). The volunteer movement provides exactly that kind of opportunity.

Dr. Tracey Jones tells the story of Louis Pasteur, considered by many the most distinguished of Frenchmen. When he was a boy his schoolteacher wrote of him, "He is the meekest, smallest and least-promising pupil in my class." At age seventy, when Pasteur was ill and too weak to go to a celebration in his honor, the son read his father's message: "The future will belong not to the conquerors, but to the saviors of mankind" (*Our Mission Today*, 137).

That same inspiration lives on today in the lives of multitudes who have been touched by the challenges of this unique ministry. Let me cite one more example. The Reverend Larry Burke of the Tennessee Conference first heard of the hurricane destruction in Jamaica some years ago, but the news did not touch him deeply at the time. The second time destruction hit the island, he was moved to join his conference's first team. His wife, Daliene, and their children were members of the second team, which he led. "That experience helped her understand the excitement I felt when I came home from my first UMVIM experience," he said. "We both were bitten by the UMVIM bug! UMVIM was both a gift from God and his method of preparing us for our future ministry as commissioned missionaries assigned to the Red Bird Missionary Conference. God could not have used a more forceful and meaningful way to call us into mission service."

The road ahead for all the jurisdictional coordinators, their staffs and fellow workers, is full of opportunity and uncertainty. Together with an excellent team of office and conference colleagues devoted to this ministry and thousands of participants across the country, this movement under God should continue to flourish.

The Reverend Nick Elliott of South Carolina, former South Carolina Conference UMVIM chair, became director of UMVIM-SEJ in July 1999.

The road UMVIM has traveled in its first two decades has surely had its ups and downs, trials and errors. Looking back to 1976 when we began our UMVIM work, I can see how my own discouragement in dealing with misunderstandings with GBGM was due to the different perspectives we held about the movement. I give thanks for the leadership that David and Mary Sue Lowry provided in that first year of this fledgling movement. From its infancy, UMVIM has continued as a truly grassroots movement in mission, often struggling just to survive. But every indication at present is that the movement has wide acceptance across the church due in part to the recognition given to UMVIM by the General Board of Global Ministries in recent years, as well as its own phenomenal growth. People at work with UMVIM can now feel confident of moving ahead with their church officially supporting them.

My own vision and prayer for the future is that God's blessing, benediction, and protection over this ministry will continue in at least the following ways:

- Persons of diverse ethnic backgrounds will participate increasingly as volunteers in mission.
- A growing number of individuals will serve from two months to two years or longer, as is already happening on a small scale.

Some may become candidates for traditional missionary service, go into other forms of Christian ministry, or choose active leadership roles as lay members in their local church.

- Church leaders in places of need will be increasingly aware of potential assistance from volunteers. This is essential as volunteers go only where invited.
- A greater emphasis will be placed on ministry to urban and rural marginalized poor, offering them the gospel and essential social services.
- An increasing number of teams of all types will develop—construction, medical, evangelism, teaching, and other specialized services—from many more churches.
- Laity and clergy will develop more maturity in the volunteer movement with greater sensitivity to the issues and the people where one seeks to serve, using this movement as one of the best instruments of mission education.
- UMVIM must be open to the guidance of the Spirit of God into new areas of service, supporting today's and tomorrow's pioneers who are confronting the many global crises.
- The number of returning volunteers will increase; they will learn the language, study the culture, serve for extended periods of time, or continue in volunteer service, returning home with greater concern about global issues beginning with their own community.
- Local churches will make more creative use of volunteers in their education, outreach, and worship programs, frequently highlighting the opportunities.
- Most important, the name of Jesus Christ will be proclaimed boldly in all aspects of mission service and witness, remembering first and foremost, the mission belongs to Christ.

As this personal account of the amazing story of this grassroots movement concludes, let me again emphasize what I consider to be the primacy of our task: to make disciples of our Lord Jesus Christ. Such was the concern of the late Bishop Ralph Ward who served many years in China. According to Tracey Jones, Bishop Ward "in Hong Kong shortly before his death in his seventy-sixth year, ordained three young Chinese men. They knelt at his bedside.

Bishop Ward was so weak that his voice was barely audible. Only with help could he sit up in bed. After placing his hands on the heads of the young men and ordaining them, he said in Chinese, 'Go preach! Go preach!' In a few moments he fell into a coma from which he never awoke. His last words are a reminder that every Christian is responsible for the people of other races and nations. This interdependence of Christians is one of the most hopeful factors to be seen within the world today" (*Our Mission Today*, 152).

Listen to this encouraging word that comes from our brother Allan Kirton, who is the principal person responsible today for training prospective missionary candidates. "In my opinion, the UMVIM movement is the greatest mission blessing with which God has endowed the church in this century. It acknowledges the mission vocation of all the people of God and fulfills the yearning of so many to participate actively." A similar statement has come also from Bishop Dan E. Solomon, president of the General Board of Global Ministries, who said simply, "Volunteers In Mission may be the salvation of The United Methodist Church."

My final word is one of thanksgiving and praise to God for raising up this grassroots movement at this strategic time in the life of the church and the world. Margaret and I have been particularly blessed and honored to be a part of this incredible ministry. And as our Caribbean Christian sisters and brothers like to say, "Let us praise God for all that is past. Let us trust God for all that is to come."

References

Allen, Roland. *Ministry of the Spirit: Selected Writings of Roland Allen.* London: World Dominion Press, 1960.

Anderson, Gerald H., ed. *Christian Mission in Theological Perspective.* Nashville: Abingdon Press, 1967.

_____ *Mission Trends,* 4 vols., Grand Rapids: Paulist Press, 1975.

Barrett, David, ed. *Unreached Peoples: Clarifying the Task.* Monrovia, Calif.: MARC, 1975.

Bassham, Rodger C. *Mission Theology: 1948–1975, Years of Worldwide Creative Tension.* Pasadena: William Carey Library, 1979.

Benjamin, Medea. *The Peace Corps and More.* San Francisco: Seven Locks Press, 1952.

Bolioli, Oscar. *The Caribbean: Culture of Resistance, Spirit of Hope.* New York: Friendship Press, 1993.

Bruton, Sheila. *Missionaries of The United Methodist Church Through the Camera's Eye.* New York: General Board of Global Ministries, 1988.

Clinton, Hillary Rodham. *It Takes a Village.* New York: Simon & Schuster, 1996.

Costas, Orlando E. *Christ Outside the Gate.* Maryknoll, N. Y.: Orbis Books, 1982.

Dayton, Edward R. and Samuel Wilson, eds. *The Refugee Among Us.* Monrovia, Calif.: MARC, 1983.

Dodge, Bishop Ralph E. *The Revolutionary Bishop.* Pasadena: William Carey Library, 1986.

Garrison, V. David. *The Nonresidential Missionary.* Monrovia, Calif.: MARC, 1990.

General Board of Global Ministries. *United Methodist Committee on Relief Handbook.* New York: General Board of Global Ministries.

González, Justo L. *Each in His Own Tongue.* Nashville: Abingdon Press, 1991.

Hopkins, Paul A. *What Next in Mission?* Philadelphia: Westminster Press, 1977.

Horne, Jean. *Unto the Least of These: Meditations for Virginia Volunteers In Mission.* Big Island, Va.: St. Andrew Press, 1989.

Ingleheart, Glenn. *Interfaith Witness: A Guide for Southern Baptists.* Richmond: Foreign Mission Board Press, 1984.

Janssen, Gretchen. *Women on the Move: A Christian Perspective in Cross-Cultural Adaptation.* Yarmouth, Maine: Intercultural Press, 1989.

Johnson, Douglas W. *Empowering Lay Volunteers.* Nashville: Abingdon Press, 1991.

Jones, Tracey K. *Our Mission Today.* New York: World Outlook Press, 1963.

_____ *The Missionary Intruder.* Nashville: Scarritt College, 1966.

Kohls, L. Robert *Survival Kit for Overseas Living.* Yarmouth, Maine: Intercultural Press, 1984.

Kroakevic, James H. and Dotsey Welliver, eds. *Partners in the Gospel.* Wheaton, Ill.: Billy Graham Center, Wheaton College, n.d.

Messer, Donald E., *A Conspiracy of Goodness: Contemporary Images of Christian Mission.* Nashville: Abingdon Press, 1992.

Moltmann, Jurgen. *The Power of the Powerless.* San Francisco: Harper & Row, 1981.

Newbigin, Lesslie. *The Gospel in a Pluralistic Society.* Grand Rapids, Mich.: Eerdmans Publishing, 1990.

Nichols, Roy C. *Footsteps in the Sea.* Nashville: Abingdon Press, 1980.

Seamands, John T. *Harvest of Humanity: The Church's Mission in Changing Times.* Wheaton, Ill.: Victor Books, 1988.

Schrock, Jan, ed. *Brethren Volunteer Service Booklet.* Elgin, Ill., 1991.

Smith, Eugene L. *Mandate for Mission.* New York: Friendship Press, 1968.

Storti, Craig. *The Art of Crossing Cultures.* Yarmouth, Maine: Intercultural Press, 1989.

Terry, Max., ed. *Volunteer! The Comprehensive Guide to Voluntary Service in the US and Abroad.* New York: Council on International Educational Exchange and the Council of Religious Volunteer Agencies, 1993.

Whiteman, Darrell. *Missiology: An International Review.* Maryknoll, N. Y.: Orbis Books, annually.

Wilson, Marlene. *How to Mobilize Church Volunteers.* Minneapolis: Augsburg, 1983.

Index